**New Directions for
Teaching and Learning**

Catherine M. Wehlburg
EDITOR-IN-CHIEF

Teaching and Learning from the Inside Out: Revitalizing Ourselves and Our Institutions

Margaret Golden
EDITOR

Number 130 • Summer 2012
Jossey-Bass
San Francisco

TEACHING AND LEARNING FROM THE INSIDE OUT:
REVITALIZING OURSELVES AND OUR INSTITUTIONS
Margaret Golden (ed.)
New Directions for Teaching and Learning, no. 130
Catherine M. Wehlburg, Editor-in-Chief

Microfilm copies of issues and articles are available in 16mm and 35mm, as well as microfiche in 105mm, through University Microfilms, Inc., 300 North Zeeb Road, Ann Arbor, MI 48106-1346.

NEW DIRECTIONS FOR TEACHING AND LEARNING (ISSN 0271-0633, electronic ISSN 1536-0768) is part of The Jossey-Bass Higher and Adult Education Series and is published quarterly by Wiley Subscription Services, Inc., A Wiley Company, at Jossey-Bass, One Montgomery Street, Suite 1200, San Francisco, CA 94104-4594. Periodicals postage paid at San Francisco, CA, and at additional mailing offices. POSTMASTER: Send address changes to New Directions for Teaching and Learning, Jossey-Bass, One Montgomery Street, Suite 1200, San Francisco, CA 94104-4594.

New Directions for Teaching and Learning is indexed in CIJE: Current Index to Journals in Education (ERIC), Contents Pages in Education (T&F), Educational Research Abstracts Online (T&F), ERIC Database (Education Resources Information Center), Higher Education Abstracts (Claremont Graduate University), and SCOPUS (Elsevier).

SUBSCRIPTIONS cost $89 for individuals and $275 for institutions, agencies, and libraries in the United States. Prices subject to change.

EDITORIAL CORRESPONDENCE should be sent to the editor-in-chief, Catherine M. Wehlburg, c.wehlburg@tcu.edu.

www.josseybass.com

CONTENTS

Editor's Notes   1
Margaret Golden

1. Principles and Practices of the Circle of Trust® Approach   3
Terry Chadsey, Marcy Jackson
The directors of the Center for Courage & Renewal discuss the principles and practices of a Circle of Trust® approach that have broad applicability across disciplines of teaching and learning.

2. Soul and Role Dialogues in Higher Education: Healing the Divided Self   15
Paul Michalec, Gary Brower
This chapter describes the creation of a university faculty–staff group formed to explore the deep heartfelt and heartbroken nature of work in academia and to develop an intentional community to discuss ways of working productively in the tension between soul and role in higher education.

3. The Circle of Trust® Approach and a Counselor Training Program: A Hand in Glove Fit   27
Judith A. Goodell
This chapter explains how the Circle of Trust principles and practices have been actively infused in a Master's of Counseling Psychology, Marriage and Family Therapy Program and issues a call for systemic reform in our institutions of higher education to embrace a model more aligned with the relational and connected world in which we live.

4. Dialing In to a Circle of Trust: A "Medium" Tech Experiment and Poetic Evaluation   37
Christine T. Love
A distance learning model in Montana uses "found poems" as an evaluative tool to provide evidence that elements of transformational learning are achievable without direct face-to-face interaction between participants.

5. The Power of Paradox in Learning to Teach   53
Karen Noordhoff
This chapter acknowledges the inherent uncertainty of both teaching and learning to teach and how learning to hold paradoxes may help teacher candidates live creatively with ambiguity.

6. The Role of Identity in Transformational Learning, Teaching, and Leading 67

Michael I. Poutiatine, Dennis A. Conners

This chapter explores the relationship between the development of identity and integrity and the process of transformation within the context of a leadership preparation program.

7. Lessons Learned from Transformational Professional Development 77

Twyla T. Miranda

A description and evaluation of a transformational professional development approach resulting in school cultures with greater relational trust and responsibility and commitment therein.

8. Circles of Learning in Mississippi: Community Recovery and Democracy Building 89

Bonnie Allen, Estrus Tucker

How an innovative community recovery and democracy building project, begun in the wake of Hurricane Katrina, offers a new approach for social change that addresses the root of human suffering lodged deep in the human heart where seeds of transformation also rest.

9. Measuring the Impact of the Circle of Trust® Approach 101

Janet Smith

This research identifies the impact of the Circle of Trust experience on the personal lives of the participants and the ways in which the experience has led to constructive action in their professional roles.

INDEX 113

FROM THE SERIES EDITOR

About This Publication

Since 1980, *New Directions for Teaching and Learning* (*NDTL*) has brought a unique blend of theory, research, and practice to leaders in postsecondary education. *NDTL* sourcebooks strive not only for solid substance but also for timeliness, compactness, and accessibility.

The series has four goals: to inform readers about current and future directions in teaching and learning in postsecondary education, to illuminate the context that shapes these new directions, to illustrate these new direction through examples from real settings, and to propose ways in which these new directions can be incorporated into still other settings.

This publication reflects the view that teaching deserves respect as a high form of scholarship. We believe that significant scholarship is conducted not only by researchers who report results of empirical investigations but also by practitioners who share disciplinary reflections about teaching. Contributors to *NDTL* approach questions of teaching and learning as seriously as they approach substantive questions in their own disciplines, and they deal not only with pedagogical issues but also with the intellectual and social context in which these issues arise. Authors deal on the one hand with theory and research and on the other with practice, and they translate from research and theory to practice and back again.

About This Volume

The work done in higher education is sometimes seen as dry, boring, and even dusty. Even though most in higher education started with feelings of hope and passion for their subject and for teaching, these feelings can sometimes be lost over time as political battles, accreditation issues, state mandates, and problems with people take center stage. This volume of *NDTL* helps to remind us that the connections we have with ourselves, our students, our colleagues, and our disciplines are truly important and meaningful—and should take precedence over these other smaller issues. By taking the work done by Parker J. Palmer and the principles and practices of the Circles of Trust approach, those in higher education can be reminded of the courage that it takes to teach and the renewal that can be generated when we live and teach more authentically in our lives, our classrooms, and in the world.

Catherine M. Wehlburg
Editor-in-Chief

CATHERINE M. WEHLBURG is the assistant provost for Institutional Effectiveness at Texas Christian University.

EDITOR'S NOTES
Providing Space for the Heart: A Structure for Transformational Teaching and Learning

Transformational teaching and learning are possible only within a space that encourages participation of the whole self—our hopes and dreams, as well as our doubts and fears. They require a space where vulnerability is valued and *not* knowing is embraced as an essential step on the learning journey. This issue explores a variety of educational initiatives that incorporate the principles and practices of a Circle of Trust® approach as developed by Parker J. Palmer and the Center for Courage & Renewal, an approach that acknowledges both the inner and outer realities of the human condition.

At the heart of each initiative described herein is the understanding that without a pedagogy that provides for both dimensions of the human experience, the value of the educational enterprise is severely diminished. We begin our exploration of these initiatives with Terry Chadsey, executive director, and Marcy Jackson, cofounder, of the Center for Courage & Renewal. They discuss how the principles and practices of a Circle of Trust® approach provide a structure for faculty and students to engage in teaching and learning that awaken both heart and mind. Each subsequent chapter illustrates these principles and practices in action through the lens of a different subject, project, or program designed to transform individuals and institutions from the inside out.

Bonnie Allen and Estrus Tucker describe how a community recovery and democracy building project in Mississippi offers a new approach to social change, one that addresses the root of human suffering. Paul Michalec and Gary Brower tell the story of creating an intentional community at the University of Denver, where faculty and staff embrace the tensions inherent in academia to remain vibrant members of their learning community. Judy Goodell, who teaches in the marriage and family therapy program at the University of San Francisco, describes the principles and practices as a "hand in glove fit" with the counselor training program there. In a teacher preparation program at Portland State University, Karen Noordhoff examines how these principles and practices help aspiring teachers appreciate the ambiguity inherent in teaching by developing an understanding of life's paradoxes. Similarly, Michael Poutiatine and Dennis Conners analyze the role of identity development in a transformational leadership program at Gonzaga University. Applying the Circle

NEW DIRECTIONS FOR TEACHING AND LEARNING, no. 130, Summer 2012 © Wiley Periodicals, Inc.
Published online in Wiley Online Library (wileyonlinelibrary.com) • DOI: 10.1002/tl.20012

of Trust pedagogy to a professional development program for K–12 educators in Texas, Twyla Miranda considers its impact on school culture and teachers' commitment to student achievement. Finally, Janet Smith evaluates the impact of the Circle of Trust® approach on the personal and professional lives of participants from a variety of programs, and Chris Love uses the novel approach of creating found poems from participant interviews to evaluate a distance-learning model. Although the context for each of these initiatives varies greatly, each consciously seeks to create a space that takes seriously what is held in the human heart, a space necessary for real transformation.

Margaret Golden, Ed.D.
Associate Professor
Director of *The Courage to Teach Initiative*
School of Education and Counseling Psychology
Dominican University of California

1

This chapter describes the history, rationale, and core content of the principles and practices that define the Circle of Trust® approach as developed by Parker J. Palmer and the Center for Courage & Renewal. Courage to Teach®, Courage to Lead®, and other Courage & Renewal programs are built upon this distinctive approach.

Principles and Practices of the Circle of Trust® Approach

Terry Chadsey, Marcy Jackson

In every discipline, knowledge is generated through a communal process. This requires habits of mind and heart that allow us to interact openly and honestly with other knowers and with the subject to be known—such habits as a capacity to care about the process, the willingness to get involved, the humility to listen, the strength to speak our truth, the willingness to change our minds. The more closely a pedagogy can emulate this communal process, cultivating these habits of mind and heart as it goes along, the deeper the learning will go.

—Parker J. Palmer, 2005

Teaching and Learning as a Communal Process

Creating a space for engaged teaching and learning has never been easy and is arguably even more challenging today with the variety and volume of external stimulation that often results in a state of "constant partial attention" for both teachers and students. Add to that the variety of teaching platforms available, from large lecture formats to small group seminars to e-courses (and all the iterations and possibilities in between), and it is easy to imagine that our previous ways of engaging minds and hearts in learning about a subject and about the world are no longer relevant.

NEW DIRECTIONS FOR TEACHING AND LEARNING, no. 130, Summer 2012 © Wiley Periodicals, Inc.
Published online in Wiley Online Library (wileyonlinelibrary.com) • DOI: 10.1002/tl.20013

Yet as Parker Palmer notes, we need to continue to find ways of learning with our whole selves—and in community with others—if we want to move beyond surface learning that is short lived. We need to engage learning and learners in ways that make it possible to deepen and transform minds and hearts. In *The Heart of Higher Education: A Call to Renewal*, Mark Nepo (2010, p. viii) puts this another way:

> What does it mean to balance educating the mind with educating the heart? In terms of action in the world, it suggests that a tool is only as good as the hand that guides it, and the guiding hand is only as wise and compassionate as the mind and heart that direct it. The heart of higher education has something to do with connecting all the meaningful parts of being human and the increasingly important challenge of how we live together in our time on earth.

Through the Center for Courage & Renewal we offer personal and professional retreats and programs designed to explore vocational and life questions, offer renewal and encouragement, and deepen engagement in professional practice. Using what we call the Circle of Trust® approach, we invite groups into a communal process based upon a set of principles and practices through which we engage our deepest questions in a way that welcomes our inwardness even as it connects us to the gifts and challenges of community and to the larger world.

To date the majority of our participants have come from K–12 and higher education settings. And although conducting our retreats is not the same as creating learning spaces for academic subjects, through these participants we have seen evidence of how elements of the Circle of Trust® approach have broad applicability to many kinds of pedagogical settings. Indeed, participants in our circles eagerly take these practices back into their classrooms and workplaces, having found them to be powerful in their own lives. In a survey by Jackson (2010), those who come from higher education settings—including many who have become Circle of Trust facilitators—regularly express how these principles and practices continue to inform and transform their teaching and leading:

> For professors, Courage & Renewal programs offer a framework for effective instruction that emerges from the heart/passion of the instructor, instead of more technical sources. Elements of Courage work is also helpful for facilitating and framing discussions in college classrooms. Courage work [also] offers a frame for hosting conversations about navigating the conflicted space between institutional imperatives (policies and protocols) which are often impersonal and the inner heart-soul of faculty and staff working in service of the institution to make it a more humane place to work and learn.
> —Paul Michalec, clinical associate professor, University of Denver

NEW DIRECTIONS FOR TEACHING AND LEARNING • DOI: 10.1002/tl

Especially in these times, encouragement and renewal are deeply needed. In teacher preparation I think the work [in Circles of Trust] is a way of providing hope and insight for new professionals. In the areas of professional development I feel that it provides teachers and administrators with opportunities for new ways of thinking about their careers and ways of mentoring others. Overall the work offers ways of sustaining the professions and the professionals. It touches the future in imaginative ways that no other work does.
—Rebecca Blomgren, dean of professional and graduate admissions, Greensboro College

Persons in universities and colleges—whether they be faculty or students—experience the same issues around identity, integrity/wholeness, and sustaining heart that [the Circle of Trust® approach] has always spoken to. In such institutions, it is often a challenge for us to remember who we are in the work we do and roles we hold.
—Karen Noordhoff, associate professor, Portland State University

In Circles of Trust our focus is on drawing out that which is found within. Although much of education is focused on transmitting information and acquiring knowledge, the intersection of that knowledge with the human heart—with one's values and life experience—is what makes learning come alive for both the teacher and the student.

In a Circle of Trust, we are invited to slow down, listen, and reflect in a quiet and focused space. At the same time, we engage in dialogue with others in the circle—a dialogue about things that matter. In large groups, in small groups, and in times for individual reflection we explore the intersection of our inner journeys and our outer lives, our work in the world and our relationships with ourselves and others.

Of course calling something a "circle of trust" does not make it so. As we have led programs and retreats for the past fifteen years we have learned something about the conditions that support the kind of inner and outer exploration noted previously. We call these the principles and practices of the Circles of Trust® approach. Together, they create the foundation for a process that is not only trustworthy but also hospitable and demanding, respectful and generative, transformative and real.

Origins of the Principles and Practices

Introductions

Some of what we love
we stumble upon—
a purse of gold thrown on the road,
a poem, a friend, a great song.
And more
discloses itself to us—

a well among green hazels,
a nut thicket—
when we are worn out searching
for something quite different.
And more
comes to us, carried
as carefully
as a bright cup of water,
as new bread.
                —Moya Cannon, *The Parchment Boat*, 1997

This may seem like an odd introduction to talking about the origins of these principles and practices, but in truth they have emerged over the years through a process of listening informed by love—love of learning and love of learners—and experiments in a pedagogy that invites the "whole person" to show up.

They have also come through experiences in communal inquiry and discernment where deep listening to one's own truth as well as that of others is valued and encouraged. This can be found in many wisdom traditions and also in particular faith communities. In this regard, a Quaker practice called the Clearness Committee—a microcosm of all that is involved in creating a safe space for one's inner truth to emerge—has been especially significant in the development of these principles and practices. Parker Palmer, in his tenure as dean of studies at Pendle Hill, a Quaker adult study center, came to understand the value of these practices and their potential for fostering deep and authentic inquiry. He began writing about their use in secular settings—highlighting the conditions necessary to safeguard and encourage such inquiry. These have become some of the core elements of the Circle of Trust® approach.

There have been various articulations of these principles and practices but the current version was crafted in 2010 by a group of Circle of Trust facilitators and Parker Palmer. Our goal was to create a clear and compelling expression of what is at the heart of this approach. In looking at them in their entirety, you will notice that any one of these principles and practices can be found in other kindred approaches. However, it is the way in which they are held together—in the hands of a skilled facilitator—that make this approach distinctive. What follows is a discussion of a few core principles and practices that have broad applicability in teaching and learning.[1]

Principles for Exploring Our Inner Lives in Community

What follows is a partial list and explication of principles taken from the Principles and Practices of the Circle of Trust® Approach document found in Appendix 1.1.

Everyone Has an Inner Teacher. Every person has access to an inner source of truth, named in various wisdom traditions as identity, true self, heart, spirit, or soul. The inner teacher is a source of guidance and strength that helps us find our way through life's complexities and challenges. Circles of Trust give people a chance to listen to this source, learn from it, and discover its imperatives for their work and their lives.

Creating the conditions that encourage the "inner teacher" to make an appearance or to be invited into dialogue in classrooms, lecture halls, and even small group seminars is not the usual fare—for students and teachers alike. In fact, in many settings such a thing would be suspect and seen as taking away from the rigor and focus on the mastery of knowledge. As teachers it asks us to trust that students have some of their own answers inside, waiting to be discovered.

An Appreciation of Paradox Enriches Our Lives and Helps Us Hold Greater Complexity. The journey we take in a Circle of Trust teaches us to approach the many polarities that come with being human as "both–ands" rather than "either–ors," holding them in ways that open us to new insights and possibilities. We listen to the inner teacher *and* to the voices in the circle, letting our own insights and the wisdom that can emerge in conversation check and balance each other. We trust both our intellects *and* the knowledge that comes through our bodies, intuitions, and emotions.

We hold open the possibility that when looked at more deeply some things that appear to be opposites hold something in common that connects them to a larger whole. In this way, we enlarge the territory of exploration and inquiry. By creating the opportunity to explore such things in dialogue with ourselves and others, we help students develop the capacity to hold the tensions inherent in their current understanding of a given subject or of our world with creativity and compassion, rather than cynicism and fear. We learn to create bridges between and among disparate ideas rather than fanning the flames of increasing polarization that is so prevalent in our world.

We Live with Greater Integrity When We See Ourselves Whole. Integrity means integrating all that we are into our sense of self, embracing our shadows and limitations as well as our light and our gifts. As we deepen the congruence between our inner and outer lives we show up more fully in the key relationships and events of our lives, increasing our capacity to be authentic and courageous in life and work.

Living with greater integrity is a lifelong journey marked by significant events and experiences that call us to act and live out of our fullest potential while also inviting an honest look at our limits, fears, and failings. Wendell Berry (1987) posits that "[t]he thing being made in a university is humanity ... [W]hat universities ... are mandated to make or to help to make is human beings in the fullest sense of those words—not just trained workers or knowledgeable citizens but responsible heirs and members of the human culture" (p. 77). Educating our students as whole people, as well as evoking their scholarship and their gifts, requires that those of us involved in guiding and instructing them work toward our own wholeness and integrity.

Practices That Encourage Shared Exploration of Self, Other, and World

What follows is a partial list and explication of practices taken from the Principles and Practices of the Circle of Trust® Approach document found in Appendix 1.1.

Creating Spaces That Are Open and Hospitable, But Resource Rich and Charged with Expectancy. In a Circle of Trust, we are invited to slow down, listen, and reflect in a quiet and focused space. At the same time, we engage in dialogue with others in the circle—a dialogue about things that matter. As this "sorting and sifting" goes on, and we are able to clarify and affirm our truth in the presence of others, that truth is more likely to overflow into our work and lives.

The key here is the combination of slowing down and creating a disciplined space for listening and learning, while also welcoming the richness and dynamic energy unleashed in a lively conversation that plumbs new depths or expands existing frontiers. This interaction between examining our own understanding and beliefs, and then testing those understandings in the crucible of an open yet focused classroom dialogue, invites and involves our whole selves in the learning exchange.

Committing to No Fixing Advising, "Saving," or Correcting One Another. Everything we do is guided by this simple rule, one that honors the primacy and integrity of the inner teacher. When we are free from external judgment, we are more likely to have an honest conversation with ourselves and learn to check and correct ourselves from within.

In order to create the kinds of spaces named earlier—where there can be a free and open exploration of a subject or a great truth—we need to let go of some of the knee-jerk reactions of academic life that can suppress deep learning. We need to learn the difference between debate and open dialogue that is receptive, not punitive or competitive. As teachers we need to find that openness first in ourselves and recognize that although we have a great store of hard-won knowledge in a particular subject, we do not have the specific answers for someone else's life. This is not only difficult to put into practice, but it is also "countercultural" to most academic (and many other) settings.

Asking Honest, Open Questions to "Hear Each Other into Speech." Instead of advising each other, we learn to listen deeply and ask questions that help others hear their own inner wisdom more clearly. As we learn to ask questions that are not advice in disguise, that have no other purpose than to help someone listen to the inner teacher, all of us learn and grow.

NEW DIRECTIONS FOR TEACHING AND LEARNING • DOI: 10.1002/tl

The practice of asking open, honest questions is at the heart of how we interact with others in a Circle of Trust. In many aspects of our lives we believe we need to be the one with the answers. We are often carefully trained to ask questions in a certain way—to be diagnostic, strategic, focused, and directive in our question asking. That way of asking questions has its place, but there is also a place for asking questions in such a way that we invite a person to voice and then listen to his or her own ideas, reflections, and formulations on the topic at hand.

The Principles and Practices at Work in the World of Education

This chapter began with Parker Palmer's premise, "In every discipline, knowledge is generated through a communal process. This requires habits of mind and heart that allow us to interact openly and honestly with other knowers and with the subject to be known." Our own experience in retreat programs and the experience of our participants suggest that the application of these principles and practices can help create such a process in higher education contexts.

Most of us have our own experiences of what Palmer describes: memories of shining moments in our own learning as students, where the integration of ourselves with the content of our learning was palpable and real. And we have memories as faculty of shining moments in facilitating the learning of others when the separations between teacher and student, researcher and subject fell away and the experience felt rich and alive. We know this happens but for most of us it is painfully rare. Too often we lose sight of the fact that teaching and learning are first and foremost deeply human processes.

Returning to the challenge to pedagogy quoted at the beginning of this chapter, "The more closely a pedagogy can emulate this communal process, cultivating these habits of mind and heart as it goes along, the deeper the learning will go." Principles and practices that are at the core of a Circle of Trust can also inform higher education settings within and between classrooms, helping faculty, student affairs professionals, and students to develop and practice those habits of heart and mind that power significant engagement and learning.

Through countless generations, human beings have been finely tuned to the rich social contexts in which learning and growth take place. We believe that the principles and practices developed in Circle of Trust programs can inform further development of pedagogy in higher education that will use and amplify the power of communal teaching and learning.

Note

1. To see the full list of principles and practices of the Circle of Trust® Approach, see Appendix 1.1.

References

Berry, W. "The Loss of the University." *Home Economics*. San Francisco: North Point Press, 1987.

Cannon, M. "Introductions." From *The Parchment Boat* by kind permission of the author and The Gallery Press, www.gallerypress.com, 1997.

Jackson, M. "Higher Education and Circles of Trust Survey." Bainbridge Isle, Wash.: Center for Courage & Renewal, 2010.

Nepo, M. "Foreword." In P. J. Palmer and A. Zajonc, *The Heart of Higher Education: A Call to Renewal*. San Francisco: Jossey-Bass, 2010.

Palmer, P. J. *A Hidden Wholeness: The Journey Toward an Undivided Life*. San Francisco: Jossey-Bass, 2004.

Palmer, P. J. "Connected Teaching & Learning." Self-published 1-page workshop handout, 2005.

TERRY CHADSEY is executive director of the Center for Courage & Renewal.

MARCY JACKSON is cofounder and senior fellow of the Center for Courage & Renewal.

Appendix 1.1

Principles and Practices of the Circle of Trust® Approach of the Center for Courage & Renewal

When people connect who they are with what they do, the seeds of transformation are planted in their lives and the lives of those they touch. When those people join with each other, transformation becomes a possibility in the larger world. Circles of Trust® support such movements toward positive personal and social change in venues ranging from the family to the workplace to the larger community.

The Circle of Trust® approach is distinguished by principles and practices intended to create a process of shared exploration—in retreats, programs, and other settings—where people can find safe space to nurture personal and professional integrity and the courage to act on it. These principles and practices are grounded in the center's core values, which spell out the foundational beliefs and intended purposes for our work with individuals, groups, and organizations.

The center takes great care to prepare facilitators who have the knowledge and skill required to hold and guide Circles of Trust using these principles and practices. These core elements, in the hands of a skilled facilitator, give this approach structure and intentionality and create its transformative power.

Principles of the Circle of Trust® Approach

> If we are willing to embrace the challenge of becoming whole, we cannot embrace it alone—at least, not for long: we need trustworthy relationships to sustain us, tenacious communities of support, to sustain the journey toward an undivided life. Taking an inner journey toward rejoining soul and role requires a rare but real form of community that I call a "circle of trust."
> —Parker J. Palmer, *A Hidden Wholeness* (adapted), 2004

Everyone Has an Inner Teacher. Every person has access to an inner source of truth, named in various wisdom traditions as identity, true self, heart, spirit, or soul. The inner teacher is a source of guidance and strength that helps us find our way through life's complexities and challenges. Circles of Trust give people a chance to listen to this source, learn from it, and discover its imperatives for their work and their lives.

Inner Work Requires Solitude and Community. In Circles of Trust we make space for the solitude that allows us to learn from within, while

---

The Center for Courage & Renewal has trademarked the name Circle of Trust® approach. This designation is for use only by Circle of Trust Facilitators who have been prepared by the center.

supporting that solitude with the resources of community. Participants take an inner journey in community where we learn how to evoke and challenge each other without being judgmental, directive, or invasive.

Inner Work Must Be Invitational. Circles of Trust are never "share or die" events but times and places where people have the freedom within a purposeful process to learn and grow in their own way, on their own schedule, and at their own level of need. From start to finish, this approach invites participation rather than insisting upon it because the inner teacher speaks by choice, not on command.

Our Lives Move in Cycles Like the Seasons. By using metaphors drawn from the seasons to frame our exploration of the inner life, we create a hospitable space that allows people of diverse backgrounds and perspectives to engage in a respectful dialogue. These metaphors represent cycles of life—such as the alternation of darkness and light, death and new life—shared by everyone in a secular, pluralistic society regardless of philosophical, religious, or spiritual differences.

An Appreciation of Paradox Enriches Our Lives and Helps Us Hold Greater Complexity. The journey we take in a Circle of Trust teaches us to approach the many polarities that come with being human as "both–ands" rather than "either–ors," holding them in ways that open us to new insights and possibilities. We listen to the inner teacher *and* to the voices in the circle, letting our own insights and the wisdom that can emerge in conversation check and balance each other. We trust both our intellects *and* the knowledge that comes through our bodies, intuitions, and emotions.

We Live with Greater Integrity When We See Ourselves Whole. Integrity means integrating all that we are into our sense of self, embracing our shadows and limitations as well as our light and our gifts. As we deepen the congruence between our inner and outer lives we show up more fully in the key relationships and events of our lives, increasing our capacity to be authentic and courageous in life and work.

A "Hidden Wholeness" Underlies Our Lives. Whatever brokenness we experience in ourselves and in the world, a "hidden wholeness" can be found just beneath the surface. The capacity to stand and act with integrity in the gap between what is and what could be or should be—resisting both the corrosive cynicism that comes from seeing only what is broken and the irrelevant idealism that comes from seeing only what is not—has been key to every life-giving movement and is among the fruits of the Circle of Trust® approach.

Practices of the Circle of Trust® Approach

In this culture, we know how to create spaces that invite the intellect to show up, to argue its case, to make its point. We know how to create spaces that invite the emotions to show up, to express anger or joy. We know how to create spaces that invite the will to show up, to consolidate effort and energy around a common task. And we surely know how to create spaces that invite the ego to show up, preening itself and claiming its turf! But we seem to know very little about creating spaces that invite the soul to show up, this core of ourselves, our selfhood.

—Parker J. Palmer, *A Hidden Wholeness*, 2004

Creating Spaces That Are Open and Hospitable, But Resource Rich and Charged with Expectancy. In a Circle of Trust, we are invited to slow down, listen, and reflect in a quiet and focused space. At the same time, we engage in dialogue with others in the circle—a dialogue about things that matter. As this "sorting and sifting" goes on, and we are able to clarify and affirm our truth in the presence of others, that truth is more likely to overflow into our work and lives.

Committing to No Fixing, Advising, "Saving," or Correcting One Another. Everything we do is guided by this simple rule, one that honors the primacy and integrity of the inner teacher. When we are free from external judgment, we are more likely to have an honest conversation with ourselves and learn to check and correct ourselves from within.

Asking Honest, Open Questions to "Hear Each Other into Speech." Instead of advising each other, we learn to listen deeply and ask questions that help others hear their own inner wisdom more clearly. As we learn to ask questions that are not advice in disguise, that have no other purpose than to help someone listen to the inner teacher, all of us learn and grow.

Exploring the Intersection of the Universal Stories of Human Experience with the Personal Stories of Our Lives. Guided conversations focused on a poem, a teaching story, a piece of music, or a work of art—drawn from diverse cultures and wisdom traditions—invite us to reflect on the "big questions" of our lives, allowing each person to intersect and explore them in his or her own way.

Using Multiple Modes of Reflection So Everyone Can Find His or Her Place and Pace. In Circles of Trust, we speak and we listen. We explore important questions in large group conversation and dialogues in small groups. We make time for individual reflection and journaling. We respect nonverbal ways of learning, including music, movement, and the arts. We honor the educative power of silence and the healing power of laughter. Together we weave a "tapestry of truth" with many and diverse threads, creating a pattern in which everyone can find a place that both affirms and stretches them.

Honoring Confidentiality. Participants in Circles of Trust understand that nothing said in these circles will be revealed outside the circle and that things said by participants will not be pursued when a session ends, unless the speaker requests it.

New Directions for Teaching and Learning • DOI: 10.1002/tl

The Principles and Practices at Work in the World

Participants in a Circle of Trust return to their homes, workplaces, and communities, taking two important resources with them: (1) greater access to the inner teacher and a new depth of self-knowledge, often resulting in a clearer sense of guidance for their personal and professional lives and a resolve to live closer to their core commitments; and (2) principles and practices from the Circle of Trust® approach that can be applied to their daily lives.

As a result of participating in circles of trust, people report:

- A stronger sense of purpose and integrity
- Expanded capacity to be fully present to others in ways that affirm and heal
- Increased skill in asking the honest, open questions that help others uncover their own inner wisdom
- Greater confidence to seek or create communities of support
- Increased understanding, appreciation, and respect for human differences, based in deeper awareness of the identity and integrity of ourselves and others
- Greater capacity to build the relational trust that helps institutions pursue their missions
- More courage to live and lead authentically
- Renewed passion for their work or vocation
- A deeper commitment to leadership and service to others

The work of the Center for Courage & Renewal and the Circle of Trust® approach is informed by a movement model of social change. Every social movement, small and large, that has made the world a more just and hospitable place has been animated by active respect for human identity and integrity. Typically, these movements have unfolded in four stages: (1) individuals reach a point where the gap between their inner and outer lives becomes so painful that they resolve to live "divided no more"; (2) people form communities of support that can help sustain that decision; (3) they go public with their values and visions in order to gather support; and (4) together in community, they achieve the moral leverage necessary to help transform our common life.

What happens in a Circle of Trust—grounded in honoring the identity and integrity of each participant—flows out into the world as an authentic source of personal and societal healing and a power for positive social change.

To learn more about the work of the Center for Courage & Renewal, visit www.couragerenewal.org. For more about the principles and practices of the Circle of Trust® approach in theory and in practice, see Parker J. Palmer, *A Hidden Wholeness: The Journey Toward an Undivided Life* (San Francisco: Jossey-Bass, 2004).

2

This chapter describes the origin of faculty–staff gatherings modeled on the Circle of Trust® approach. It outlines the structure of the meetings, offers descriptions of participant experiences, and ends with suggestions for ways of hosting similar gatherings on other college campuses.

Soul and Role Dialogues in Higher Education: Healing the Divided Self

Paul Michalec, Gary Brower

A group of faculty and staff gather in a conference room in the student union to share experiences with the soul–role divide at work and in the classroom. They sit around a table of natural wood with inlaid geometric patterns made from an eclectic assortment of colorful woods. The walls of the room are painted in earth tones and adorned with large-scale photographs of mountains. The meeting begins with a reminder of the group's conversational norms that invite deep reflection and a safe place for the soul. The facilitator reviews the topic for the meeting by telling a brief personal story relevant to the theme. A poem with accompanying journal prompts is distributed and read out loud. Several minutes of silence follow as each participant underlines words, circles passages, or writes margin notes on the poem, as everyone moves into a familiar and comfortable sense of being present with each other. The facilitator opens with a question inviting participants to share stories of personal meaning emerging from the poem. For the next hour the discussion moves back and forth between the poem, shared examples of personal meaning, and increased understanding of the depth and productive power of the soul–role divide in higher education. The purpose of the meeting is exploring the deep heartfelt and heartbroken nature of work in academia, developing a sense of the shared journey, and examining ways of working productively in the tension between soul and role in higher education.

This chapter describes the origin of these staff–faculty gatherings, outlines the structure of the meetings, offers descriptions of participant

New Directions for Teaching and Learning, no. 130, Summer 2012 © Wiley Periodicals, Inc.
Published online in Wiley Online Library (wileyonlinelibrary.com) • DOI: 10.1002/tl.20014

experiences, and ends with suggestions for ways of hosting similar gatherings on other college campuses. In September 2008, Parker Palmer, the noted author and educational reformer, visited our campus to speak on the topic of K–12 school reform. Both authors of this chapter were active members of the planning committee that hosted an array of small-group discussions, formal presentations, and lectures by Palmer. Throughout the length of his stay it became increasingly clear to us that there was more we could do to engage the campus community in continued dialogue around personal meaning and purpose for staff, faculty, and administrators. To that end, in the winter and spring of 2009 we invited a group of faculty and staff to attend a monthly discussion called "soul–role dialogues." The meetings were sponsored by the chaplain's office, under the leadership of Gary Brower, and designed by Paul Michalec, a trained Courage to Teach® facilitator and faculty member. Both Gary and Paul facilitated the discussion throughout the academic year.

Our planning was informed by the energy that Parker Palmer's visit brought to campus as well as the existing literature on spirituality in higher education (Astin, Astin, and Lindholm, 2005; Chickering, Dalton, and Stamm, 2005; Palmer and Zajonc, 2010). What we noticed in the literature on spiritual development in higher education, particularly the Astin, Astin, and Lindholm (2005) report, was the divide between personal commitments to spiritual development and the limited visible presence of spirituality on campus. As noted by Astin, Astin, and Lindholm, "more than half (56%) of the students in the survey say that their professors never provide opportunities to discuss the meaning and purpose of life. Similarly, nearly two-thirds (62%) say professors never encourage discussion of spiritual or religious matters" (p. 1). Meanwhile, the same survey reports that "nearly half of today's faculty (47 percent) believe that 'integrating spirituality in my life' is an essential or very important life goal" (p. 3). Palmer and Zajonc (2010) trace this separation of the personal and the role of professor to an "incorrect conceptual map of the academy and the place of spirituality within it" (p. 118). In particular they cite the ways the map sets "science and religion in opposition to each other" (p. 118). One antidote to this flawed theoretical framework for organizing knowledge is to convene what Palmer (2009) describes as "circles of trust" where groups of faculty come together under skilled leadership to share stories of teaching that reveal the inner wisdom of the teacher through community. And it is often during these conversations that a sense of "hidden wholeness" emerges that rejoins soul and role.

By "soul" we mean a sense of deep calling to the work of higher education, an abiding presence of inner calm and passion for the work, and a universal sense of longing to belong to the communal pursuit of some ideal or concept greater than oneself. This call to holism, we believe, is one of the driving forces behind the liberal arts tradition in higher education, and on our campus it is evident in the college motto: "Start from a higher place." By "role" we mean the institutional niche or niches that a person fits.

Both halves (soul and role), when they are present in the daily work world of individuals, are best perceived as separate but equal elements of a person's institutional identity. But when they are at odds with each other the more visible and demanding institutional role often quiets the voice of the less evident and more humble soul. The tension between soul and role, if left unattended, can lead to a loss of personal integrity and authenticity resulting in what Palmer (2007) calls the "divided self." If the soul–role divide continues for an extended period of time, the work environment can begin to take on qualities of disenchantment, loss of heart, and burnout.

Soul–Role Dialogues

It was our hope that the soul–role dialogues would temper the caustic nature of the divided self and reposition the soul and role as necessary equals in the institutional life of faculty, staff, and administrators. We structured the monthly meetings, over the course of the year, around a theme generated from our wider sense of the challenges of academic life, the metaphor of the seasons in the natural-professional world (Palmer, 2007), or particular concepts gleaned from the previous monthly soul–role dialogue. The types of themes we examined included identity, preparing for the work, winter's dormancy at work, and abundance.

Each monthly meeting was bounded by ground rules for interaction, a poem selected to invite deep meaning and conversation around a particular theme, and journal prompts to encourage personal understanding of the soul–role conflict at work. The norms were open enough to invite meaningful sharing around soul–role conflicts and structured enough to keep the discussion moving toward sources of inner wisdom rather than wandering off into the terrain of professional griping and discontent about work. Drawing on Paul's work as a nationally prepared Courage to Teach® facilitator, we offered the group the set of guidelines for discussion outlined in Appendix 2.1.

Poetry was ideal for the task of opening up the self to inner wisdom because of its ability to raise universal themes while also supporting personal meaning making. Palmer (2007) refers to this aspect of poetry as a poetic Rorschach test, where each reader sees and hears unique words, images, and phrases that resonate with the personal condition of the soul. In this way, we had a text that everyone read through the lens of a common theme, while also paying close attention to questions of personal meaning.

In addition to the norms and the poem, we also included three to four journal prompts as intellectual-heart starters for conversation. The prompts were intended to draw the attention of participants to particular subthemes in the poem, rather than to be directive and suggestive of a "right" way to respond to the challenges of productively holding the tension between soul and role.

A week before each gathering we e-mailed the participants the norms, the meeting agenda including a brief description of the theme, the poem, and journal prompts. (See Appendix 2.1 for an example.) At the start of our meeting we typically sat in silence for several minutes, waiting for the busyness of the mind and ego to calm and quiet, a sort of emotional–intellectual settling. The silence is followed by a reminder of the norms for being together and a short framing of the theme, typically in the form of a personal story that exemplifies in concrete terms elements of the soul–role conflict for the month. The poem is read out loud and a general invitation is extended to share words, images, or phrases that captured the heart's attention. If warranted, the facilitator might ask participants to journal on one or more of the prompts.

Participant Experiences

In the following section we offer vignettes of five different participants highlighting their experience and outcomes with the soul–role conversations. The five stories feature the voices of an administrator, a staff person, a pretenured faculty, a tenured faculty, and an adjunct faculty member of the university. All five stories were fact checked with participants for accuracy and meaning. By telling these stories it is possible to see the potential for wider impact of soul–role conversations on other campuses. Later we offer our analysis of the vignettes and suggest ways that soul–role dialogues could enhance campus climate and collegiality across many campuses.

Vignette One: University Administrator. Dave participated in the soul–role dialogues because he feels that some "privacy and legal barriers" in higher education "create a perception that there are things that can't be spoken of openly." For Dave, one of the taboo topics is spirituality, a subject in which he would like to more fully engage his students. But he holds back because the norms of academia encourage him to "bracket his identity" and interaction with students, which "creates a problem of authenticity."

He attended the soul–role conversations because they "provided an opportunity to explore authenticity on a person to person level." Dave found the dialogues so valuable to his personal and professional growth that he "made space in his calendar" even though he felt constrained by the "busy" feeling of the campus and his "immediate work load." To that end, the dialogues "took the pressure off of the pressure cooker of work" by creating for Dave a "structure that was safe and private which created a sense of liberty and freedom" to talk about things that were harder to share in other areas of Dave's professional life. Key to this outcome were the poems, which he found "very compelling and invited me to dig deeper."

NEW DIRECTIONS FOR TEACHING AND LEARNING • DOI: 10.1002/tl

For Dave, the long-term impact of participation was a sense of being "opened up to be more hospitable to other people" in his role as an administrator. He "hopes" that there will be a "continuation of these conversations and exploration of how to encourage openness on campus." Dave believes that "there is too much stridency and polarization on campus," and he senses that "broader" participation in soul–role dialogues might defuse this polarization and create a more open campus climate.

Vignette Two: Program Staff. Where Dave's soul feels less welcome at work, Jasmine feels that "there are not a lot of things that violate my soul." In her work life she "feels blessed that [her] soul isn't often compromised" as a staff person. Although living divided was less prevalent for Jasmine, she was drawn to the soul–role dialogues for "three reasons: one, an opportunity to meet others since I'm isolated on campus within my building; two, I've always been interested in poetry and this approach to understanding poetry; and three, an opportunity for deep meaningful conversations with colleagues." For Jasmine the dialogues were "a refreshing and safe space in the middle of the day." She felt strongly that "the process spoke right to [her]."

Given her reasons for attending, it is not surprising that Jasmine connected with poetry as a tool for meaning making, which she describes as a "chance to explore the themes I was working on personally [and] professionally." And true to the power of poetry to open up new ways of seeing truth, the poems provided language and structure "to experience what is inexpressible." Four poems had particular meaning for Jasmine: "Old Maps," "The Seven of Pentacles," "Sweet Darkness," and "The Woodcarver."

In addition to the poems, the soul–role dialogues supported a communal space where "the rich interactions with others opened up avenues of understanding that wouldn't have otherwise been possible." She marveled that the collegial nature of the dialogue created "the opportunity to see different perspectives and sharing ideas" and that this type of discourse could be achieved in an academic setting "without the discussion being threatening or conflict ridden." True to her sense that the soul–role dialogues were about building new relationships on campus, Jasmine felt that she would "come away from the meetings being connected to others and enriched in ways that typically don't happen on campus."

Although she made a personal commitment to attend all the dialogues, she experienced challenges fulfilling her intention, including "personal challenges, feeling intensely introverted, and sometimes [she] didn't have a work related tension to share or one that [she] didn't want to share at that time."

Vignette Three: Pretenured Faculty. Of high priority to Erin in this stage of her career is assembling her tenure file. Given the tensions and challenges she currently experiences as pretenured faculty, it is little wonder that she defined soul–role conflicts as "mostly related to trying to find a way to succeed in my career while feeling connected to my larger 'vocation' and not losing my soul to the institution's demands and constant press of tasks." For Erin, one strategy for blunting the institutional impulse to divide the soul from the role is "building a community here that has some sort of spiritual connection." The soul–role dialogues were an important aspect of nurturing her soul with the help of colleagues while also attending to the demands of tenure at the university.

Like Dave and Jasmine, Erin found that she "got something out of [the poems]" and she "saved 'Rebus' as I found it very enriching and I also remember the Mary Oliver poem on geese." The poetry provided a center of meaning for Erin in the midst of the challenges and uncertainties of her pretenure review: "The greatest impacts were the few moments of sanity and deep conversation with other souls here at the university. I loved musing together on something and just getting away from the constant stress I feel as a pretenure person." The shared dialogues supported Erin's sense of personal wholeness as they "pulled two aspects of my life together: my spiritual life, which I pursue at a church and in meditation and prayer, and my teaching–writing life here at the university."

Erin was renewed from the "few moments of sanity and deep conversation with other souls" that the soul–role dialogues provided. But like Jasmine, she too was challenged by other time commitments: "When do we ever have 'extra' time? I often thought I could make it and then had something 'more pressing' come up."

Vignette Four: Tenured Faculty. Beth, as a senior faculty and program coordinator, experiences many of the soul-dividing institutional pressures that Erin, as a junior faculty, also faces: "I got interested [in the soul–role dialogues] because I felt a split [in my work]. I knew how to do parts of my job but other parts were more difficult. I couldn't write. I was frozen, tapped, and I didn't know what to do." Her struggles with writing, a defining craft skill for a professor, fueled an emerging sense of wonder around the potential of "being a failed academic." Beth gravitated toward the communal nature of the soul–role dialogue as a way to help rekindle her love of academia and unite her divided self: "I loved the idea of talking about the soul–role conflict at my work place where my role is split." And like other participants in the dialogues she "had hopes for a new community where I could meet new people."

For Beth, the dialogues seemed to lessen the impulse of work to divide soul from role in her daily life as a professor: "These gatherings helped me gain perspective, to not get so caught up in my stuff. They helped me see the university as a place to get nourished and not just work like a dog. And they helped me remember to pay attention to the seasons. I started gardening again to be in touch with the seasons: birth, death, growth and it begins all again." For Beth, her work now contained moments of healing instead of being only a source of uncertainty and personal divisiveness.

Poetry was an important voice of wisdom and role model for responding to the soul–role conflicts in Beth's professional life. Mary Oliver's poem,

"Wild Geese," seemed to offer Beth a way forward through her soul–role troubles: "'Wild Geese' really spoke to me. It gave me permission not to walk on my knees and to open up and enjoy life, holding it as a beautiful thing, to be part of the connection to nature and the larger world. It was a model of the expansiveness of a good poem."

The soul–role dialogues were an important element in Beth's process for understanding her writer's block and reengaging her scholarship in meaningful ways. Yet her work demands could be so deenergizing that one more task, even a meeting that fostered healing, was sometimes one task too many for Beth: "When faced with the choice of staying later or going home, the choice was easy." And even when she was energized enough to attend she found it challenging to bridge the contrasting nature of the soul-opening space of the dialogues with the role-demanding nature of work: "It was hard to switch gears from work mode to being more open and vulnerable." And finally, even though she gained personally from the dialogues, she found "it was hard to take time for self, to go and allow myself to be more open. It is like going to the gym. It was hard to open up but once I was there, at the meeting, it was great."

Many of the soul–role participants, including Beth, experienced institutional demands that could push against the nurturing, affirming, and healing nature of the dialogues. Yet, Beth and her colleagues kept coming back for the "spiritual nourishment and sense that I had done something at work that was good for me and refreshed my spirit. Outside of my classroom teaching, work is not so nourishing. It is a lot of labor with little reward. The fact that these meetings were a source of renewal while at work was great."

Vignette Five: Adjunct Faculty. Clare was attracted to the idea of the soul–role dialogues after hearing Parker Palmer's address to the university. Her interest led to her involvement in the planning team for the dialogues and she regularly attended meetings until she left her position at the university. For Clare, the soul–role dialogues provided an opportunity to discern whether her personal values were in sync with her position or if the separation of soul and role would limit her ability to be fully present and authentic to herself and others at work. Because she was an adjunct faculty, her ties to the university were more tenuous than those of the other participants in this study. Yet the soul–role dialogues were life giving and offered enough potential for self-growth that she committed energy both to starting the dialogues and attending meetings throughout her employment at the university.

As Clare wrestled with the question of staying or leaving her position, the soul–role dialogues provided support and safety as she considered her next steps. This was the case even though she never shared the depth of her internal struggles with the group. Just being present in the dialogues, without the pressure of having to contribute, brought a deep richness to her internal process of meaning making. The Marge Piercy poem, "The Seven of Pentacles," offered the greatest insight on her challenges. The image of a gardener tilling the soil and being patient for the outcome helped frame her thinking about her position and her decision to leave and till a new professional field.

Implications and Considerations

The five soul–role participants featured in this chapter share many similar experiences and rewards, even though they represent a wide range of institutional roles. All experienced some aspect of the divided self as the institutional pressures they faced drove a wedge between their soul and role. Sometimes the split was easily mended and at other times the divide seemed to threaten their institutional life and sense of well-being, even to the point of deciding to leave the university. Common themes across all five participants included an interest in finding ways of infusing spirituality more fully into institutional roles; a desire to build community through the sharing of stories of the divided self; embracing poetry as a useful tool for seeing truth where deep uncertainty once stood; and the unexpected challenges of fitting the heart-mending soul–role dialogues into their busy academic and professional schedules.

What the soul–role dialogues clearly provided for all of these individuals was an opportunity to explore and perhaps breach the wall of separation that our contemporary society and university life have erected between what we *do* and who we *are*. Such a divide—albeit in a different context—is documented in Donna Freitas's (2008) book, *Sex and the Soul*. Freitas describes how college students negotiate the tensions between their religious beliefs and their relationship struggles, specifically their sexual behavior. And she points out that, for many, those two aspects of their lives are completely compartmentalized, illustrating one example of ways that "soul" and "role" are seen as separate, not integral conversation partners.

For faculty, there is often a hesitancy to reveal their passion (soul) about their subject matter in the classroom, for fear of violating the supposed "objective" nature of a university education. Yet students often want and need that kind of perspective to make full sense of the course material. Students' understanding is often bound up in knowing the answers to a few simple questions: "*Why* would an instructor devote herself to such an arcane subject? What drives her to study it?"

If students do not see passion and its counterpart—integration— among their intellectual elders, how will they learn to practice it and become more fully authentic, present, and whole as learners? As the five vignettes of soul–role dialogue participants suggest, such authenticity (soul–role integration), is rarely encouraged or pursued in higher education. Given the potential for soul–role healing we witnessed on our campus, we will continue the dialogues and look for ways to blunt the institutional demands that often limit participation. This chapter suggests

NEW DIRECTIONS FOR TEACHING AND LEARNING • DOI: 10.1002/tl

that it is possible, in a few hours each month, to foster healthier individuals and institutional life through poetry and silent-communal reflection around original purposes and current tensions.

References

Astin, A. W., Astin, H. S., and Lindholm, J. A. *Spirituality and the Professoriate: A National Study of Faculty Beliefs, Attitudes, and Behaviors.* Los Angeles: Higher Education Research Institute, Graduate School of Education & Information Studies, University of California, Los Angeles, 2005. http://spirituality.ucla.edu/docs/results/faculty/spirit_professoriate.pdf.

Chickering, W., Dalton, J., and Stamm, L. *Encouraging Authenticity and Spirituality in Higher Education.* San Francisco: Jossey-Bass, 2005.

Freitas, D. *Sex and the Soul: Juggling Sexuality, Spirituality, Romance, and Religion on America's College Campuses.* New York: Oxford University Press, 2008.

Palmer, P. *The Courage to Teach: Exploring the Inner Landscape of a Teacher's Life.* 10th Anniversary Edition. San Francisco: Jossey-Bass, 2007.

Palmer, P. *A Hidden Wholeness: The Journey Toward an Undivided Life.* San Francisco: Jossey-Bass, 2009.

Palmer, P., and Zajonc, A. *The Heart of Higher Education: A Call to Renewal.* San Francisco: Jossey-Bass, 2010.

Paul Michalec is associate clinical professor and director of Teacher Education Programs in the Morgridge College of Education, University of Denver.

Gary Brower is university chaplain at the University of Denver.

New Directions for Teaching and Learning • DOI: 10.1002/tl

Appendix 2.1

*Soul and Role Touchstones

- Bring 100% of self
- There is always invitation, always opportunity; never invasion
- No fixing, no saving, and no advising
- Openness to learning from others
- Speak for yourself; tell your story
- Listen to the silence
- Confidentiality

Sample Soul and Role agenda

Soul and Role (November, 2011)

Introductions:

- Name, role, and favorite fall memory?

Touchstones:

- Reminder of our norms for creating a container for our time together

Today's Theme:

- Current condition of your work world; soul and role
- Poetry as the truth told at a slant, storytelling of one's selfhood
- "Panning" as a metaphor for what it feels like to gain new insights about self as a result of being sloshed around at work by forces external to oneself
- Finding ways to turn adversity into golden nuggets of self knowledge

Reflective Dialogue:

- What word image or phrase captured your attention around the theme of using the ebb and flow of work to reveal core inner qualities of self?
- Journal prompts that grabbed the attention of your heart?
- Other noticings

Closing:

- What would you like to carry from this gathering back to your work world at DU?

Journal prompts

1. Have you ever felt sloshed around in your work; unable to remain centered for an extended period of time? How have you made sense of that feeling? What did you attribute that sense of disequilibrium to?

---

*Modified from the Courage to Teach® touchstones; Center for Courage & Renewal.

New Directions for Teaching and Learning • DOI: 10.1002/tl

2. What is lost when the waters of your work slosh over the edge?
3. What is left behind that is worth re-examining for the gold of your work? Are there any new insights or golden nuggets of self knowledge left behind as a result of the panning process in work?
4. How might you take your newly discovered sense of inner strength and wisdom and apply this knowledge to your work?

3

This chapter describes how the principles and practices of a Circle of Trust® approach are infused into the Master's in Counseling Psychology program, marriage and family therapy emphasis, at the University of San Francisco. The interface between the Circle of Trust® approach and other on-campus activities is described; the model is proposed as of value to all in higher education independent of role or discipline.

The Circle of Trust® Approach and a Counselor Training Program: A Hand in Glove Fit

Judith A. Goodell

Counselor training programs are charged with developing in students the skills needed for assisting clients through processes of reformation in their lives. Counselors guide clients in responding to the events of their lives; they facilitate behavior change and offer problem-solving strategies. Counselors challenge clients to choose processes of growth over disintegration. They offer support as clients create new dreams and make new meaning of the themes in their lives.

The Circle of Trust® approach (www.couragerenewal.org) is dedicated to principles and practices that support exploration of the inner landscape of one's life. Participants share time in a trustworthy environment, connect with inner wisdom, and seek harmony in their personal and professional selves. In this chapter, I describe my experience of wearing the dual hats of professor in a counselor training program and facilitator of Courage & Renewal programs. I suggest the Circle of Trust® approach and counselor training programs are a hand in glove fit. I describe the infusion of Courage practices into the Counseling Psychology MA program, marriage and family therapy (MFT) emphasis, at the University of San Francisco (USF); its value for school counselors has been addressed previously (Goodell and Robinson, 2008). Finally, I propose the Circle of Trust® approach has much to offer in all higher education, independent of role or discipline.

New Directions for Teaching and Learning, no. 130, Summer 2012 © Wiley Periodicals, Inc.
Published online in Wiley Online Library (wileyonlinelibrary.com) • DOI: 10.1002/tl.20015

Historically, when the profession of psychotherapy and counseling emerged, classically trained therapists maintained remote personal relationships with their patients. Humanistic models then evolved and an active, empathic client–counselor relationship became central. Although counselor technique is important, it must be grounded in a caring relationship (Edwards and Bess, 1998). The field of counseling is constantly growing and changing. Because it is still tied to the medical model, the profession remains committed to diagnosis of what is "wrong" and to alleviating symptoms. The *Diagnostic and Statistical Manual of Mental Disorders IV TR* (2000) continues to uphold a diagnostic standard: treatment of disorders is the work of therapists and counselors. Licensure exams require these skills; it is a reductionistic system that has been in place for years.

Newer theories, which focus on strengths assessment and cultivation of positive attributes, continue to evolve, suggesting that good counseling occurs with a broader brushstroke. Positive psychology emphasizes minimizing what is wrong while simultaneously strengthening what is already present and working in the life of the client (Snyder and Lopez, 2002). Gratitude and forgiveness work, once considered the domain of spiritual direction, are now researched therapeutic processes (Luskin, 2002; Seligman, 2002). Counseling increasingly involves integration of mind, body, and spirit.

Traditional reductionistic theories are questioned as insufficient. Bussolari and Goodell (2009) suggest that Chaos theory is a useful tool counselors can employ when working with clients who are facing life changes across time. Nonlinear dynamics add a helpful perspective, for the typical human life rarely unfolds in systematically planned ways.

The licensing board for California Marriage and Family Therapists is mandating a revision of all training programs by 2012. Changes include increased emphasis on positive psychological strategies and focus on a recovery model dedicated to the highest quality of life possible for clients' unique situations. The profession continues to move toward a model that tends to the whole person and his or her challenges and strengths. The counseling relationship is the arena in which that work is done.

Counselor training attends to the interior development of the counselor, for it is that person who guides and supports clients in their journey to attain a higher quality of life. A counselor is unlikely to move clients in directions they cannot themselves imagine exploring. Many professions, like carpenters, surgeons, and plumbers, create success in their relationship with their tools. In these professions relationships with customers, though valuable, may not be central. This is not the case with our counselors—we need clients to meet us in the context of a solid caring relationship. We expect them to have examined their own developmental story.

The counselor's person is a major tool of their trade. Although volumes have been written on how counseling works, much research suggests the counselor–client relationship is a primary variable in the efficacy of counseling (Aron, 1996; Edwards and Bess, 1998; Levitt, Butler, and Hill, 2006; Lewis, Amini, and Lannon, 2000; Wampold, 2001). Counselors must, therefore, attend carefully to inner landscapes of their own lives, examine their places of unfinished business, and be aware of their strengths and limitations. They must paradoxically know their own story while allowing it to rest in the background as they attend fully to that of the client.

Palmer (1998) has eloquently stated that it is the self who teaches that is central to good teaching. The belief that we all hold a deep inner core of wisdom is central to the Circle of Trust® approach. It is a hand in glove fit, then, to extend this belief to the training of the "counselor as a person." The core place of the self who counsels and our capacity to show up in trustworthy relationships is the foundation of our success as counselors.

Infusion of Circle of Trust Principles and Practices into the USF MFT Program

Following my training as a facilitator, it seemed natural and beneficial to infuse Circle of Trust principles and practices into my work with the USF MFT program. Because I am committed to developing my own soul and role partnerships, it made sense that my Circle of Trust training would interface with my on-campus teaching and program coordination. My two roles elicited different environmental formats; my inner person worked at remaining consistent. This section describes ways in which I have actively incorporated the Circle of Trust® approach into five classes I currently teach in the counseling psychology program.

The strategies I identify are not new. New applications invite old practices forward to assist budding counselors in reconnecting with their own developmental story, their hopes, dreams, and fears. The Circle of Trust® approach facilitates reflection of the self and the self in relationship to others. There is invitation to the counselor to integrate soul and new role.

The MFT program at USF contains four foundation perspectives: an emphasis on lifelong development, multicultural aspects, short-term problem-solving therapy, and a family systems model. These perspectives are found throughout the courses. Instructors emphasize traditional evidence-based strategies where behavior change and problem-solving skills can be helpful to a client. When adaptation to change and life's transitions are the client's work, and where the need to make meaning out of one's existence becomes central, Circle of Trust practices help to provide a map through difficult terrain. The universal languages embedded in "third things" (like poetry and music) help clients feel less alone; stories remind us of our shared humanity.

Individual and Family Development across the Lifespan is a first-semester class in which students immerse themselves in the study of the human life and reconnect with their own unique story. Academic discussion of issues such as abuse, poverty, bullying, and family mental illness often raises strong emotions in students. Circle of Trust practices offer students a way to approach academic topics through a different lens. More important, these practices facilitate the inner work of the students because they offer tools for integrating emotions and thoughts around all aspects of human experience; tough topics and not-yet experienced aspects of life are not walled off into mental boxes to be considered by only the "head." Students have an open invitation to continue their own work of personal integration. Consistent with recent research identifying the value of embracing vulnerability (Brown, 2010), fear and vulnerability are invited into the classroom to be examined and managed in life-affirming ways. Third things enrich this exploration; students reflect on poems related to both difficult and high points in their lives. Poets and musicians bring the universal meanings and unique experiences of each stage of life to the forefront of classroom dialogue.

Circle of Trust touchstones, or group agreements, are adapted as a bridge for personal reflection. After students deliver a presentation in an assigned small group, the touchstones help them reflect upon the experience with questions such as, "When the going gets tough, how do you cope?" or "To what degree did you find yourself extending welcome—or not—to other group members?" The touchstones guide students in examining their own response to being in relationship with others—a prerequisite to being able to effectively help others examine similar issues. The touchstones are particularly useful in this class as a "perspective-extender." Budding counselors must relinquish their attachment to their own view as "correct" and learn to sit with the paradox of holding many versions of a current "truth."

The Group Therapy and Leadership class is designed to teach students skills for facilitating therapeutic, psychoeducational, and consulting groups. Students colead sessions in which all classmates are group participants, including me. This is not group therapy; each week a new theory is demonstrated. However, participants may engage at a deep personal level with their own story, so the ongoing process can become a circle of trust—or not. To create a trustworthy foundation for this process, I facilitate the first demonstration and use a circle of trust to do so. Effort is given to declaring the voluntary nature of participation in the circle itself, consistent with the Circle of Trust principle that such work is invitational. The touchstones are used as the model for creating group structure and the rule of double confidentiality is invoked. Confidentiality is essential. Students appreciate assurance that, once out of the circle, the personal content they shared will not be spoken of again.

My experience has been that using the Circle of Trust® approach in this first group demonstration creates a strong potential for ongoing safety for the entire semester. The touchstones, use of third things, and the reflective nature of the experience set a tone that is respectful and encouraging. Most students use their confidential logs to report fears they had upon entering the class; for example, some students may fear exposure or inadequacy. The Circle of Trust® approach appears to be a strong bridge between the academic setting and the possibility of honest trustworthy interpersonal circle experiences. Students can share in a common experience, drop façades of trying to "look good," and trust that the setting will allow a potentially meaningful experience. The Circle of Trust® approach is a powerful stage setter that encourages students in their coming facilitation experiences.

Individual and Family Life Transitions Counseling is a skill-based class where Circle of Trust practices are at home. The universal art of storytelling serves as a foundation in this course. Students learn that it is the stories people create about events in their lives that define their subsequent responses. Working with life transitions involves guiding people through the transitional processes put in place when a change occurs. Stories and story creation assist in adaptation and possible transformation as clients lean into change and the corner-turning events in their lives. The selective use of poetry, music, and image assists people in creating new meaning in their lives; increasing a sense of connectedness to all humanity helps people heal.

The Life Transitions class focuses on facilitating adaptation as people move through transition. Traditional interventions are taught to be used when needed. However, it is important for students to know that when behavior change and problem solving are done, our transitions often continue to leave us in places of loss and confusion. Third things help clients to locate their experience in the fabric of their lives. Many life transitions involve changes in the story we hold, and the Circle of Trust® approach has much to offer in the area of meaning making. Storytelling assists the client in grieving what has been lost and embracing the gifts of the new place, relationship, or experience (Dingfelder, 2011). Third things help create new meaning, which enhances quality of life. Poetry, in particular, is gifted as a universal language (Fox, 1997; Gladding, 1979). Poetry speaks of our shared human experiences of brokenheartedness, grief, dealing with obstacles, loneliness, and defining hopes and dreams for the future. It provides clients with a bridge to their next place in life.

In Traineeship I and Traineeship II classes, second-year students share their current four-hundred-hour field placement experiences. Traineeship classes are highly clinical and primarily involve case review. Each week students present cases and receive feedback. As they grapple with trying to help clients, emerging clinicians must make it a priority to continue to track their own "counselor as a person" process. It is common for strong thoughts and feelings to surface as students enter the field of clients and their stories for the first time. Fear, doubts, feelings of inadequacy, anger, and hopelessness enter the classroom as students talk about powerful client interactions. Carefully selected third things help integrate the personal and professional experiences of the student. Each Traineeship I and II class ends with a shared reading of a selected poem; the formation questions I offer invite students to consider the impact of the week's themes upon their personal and professional selves. The following class begins with an invitation to vocalize those reflections. Sharing is voluntary and does not affect a student's academic grade. Students report this personal reflection as important in their process of integrating their own soul and role. It also models how one might incorporate use of third things with individual clients. As each semester proceeds, it is typical for students to share case reviews that incorporate powerful use of third things with clients, individually and in groups.

The Circle of Trust® Approach and Other On-Campus Activities

In my role as professor, I have other opportunities to share Circle of Trust practices with faculty, staff, and students. Examples of these diverse experiences follow. The Catholic Educational Leadership (CEL) Program is embedded into the larger Department of Leadership Studies at USF; it is devoted to Ed.D. and MA degree programs for educators in Catholic education. In 2007, during the summer session referred to as SummerWest, I was invited to do a five-day, one-unit class embodying the Circle of Trust® approach titled The Spirit of the Educator.

Catholic educators and administrators from as far away as the East Coast and Guam participated in this Circle of Trust format. Although one academic unit was awarded for participation in the four hours per day, weeklong experience, the format was that of a retreat. Students came into a circle daily and were guided by formation questions that assisted them in examining their current personal and professional journey. This diverse group, which included members of religious life and lay persons working in Catholic settings, found the confidential circle to be a place for deep sharing and reflection.

One school principal had witnessed the destruction of Hurricane Katrina, the demolition of schools, and loss of lives. He was given the task of assisting in reforming educational settings while also attempting to manage his own grief, frustration, and anger around the tragedy. Another participant had grown through the educational ranks in Guam and now held leadership responsibilities for island students who demonstrated widely diverse needs. A third participant, relatively new to religious life, found himself dealing for the first time with his family stories of being adrift at sea as refugees. Other people I met at SummerWest included lay leaders from differing urban and suburban locations, each with their own unique challenges. Though circle members could not have been more different in background and current assignments, the week we all spent in a trustworthy circle afforded each member a deep sharing of their stories and a further discovery of our common humanity. One member described it well. At the closing of the circle he indicated that he arrived on the first day, found a place in the circle, and opened his computer. Within fifteen minutes he realized he was about to engage in something different and closed his computer for the week. This one-unit experience was part of the rich gathering of electives, each emphasizing elements of developmental and applied spirituality. The Circle of Trust fit well within this SummerWest menu in both content and format.

The next story comes from the Dual Degree program for teachers at the University of San Francisco. Each term new students entered the program hoping to receive a teacher's credential and a subject specialization. For many years, I provided a one-time brown bag seminar introducing the Circle of Trust® approach as part of the students' early program support. The director hoped their brief experience with the formation activities would encourage them to hold a belief that it is the person who teaches that is core. Participants were given Circle of Trust information for future reference.

This final example relates to an on-campus group termed "Spirituality in the Workplace." It was formed through a word-of-mouth process and included faculty, staff, and administrators who felt the need for a communal way to share their own formation process. This group met monthly for a midday, two-hour period. Each month one member facilitated a third thing experience. A Circle of Trust setting was used; participants respected the timing, setting, and activities. Three members were familiar with Circle of Trust retreats. The group was a grounding and renewing experience for participants. Unfortunately, it dissolved after two years when a handful of participants moved away. A new potential version is being explored by a group of cross-campus faculty members who are interested in principles of meditative teaching.

The Circle of Trust® Approach for Educators in Changing Times

We are educators in challenging times. Palmer and Zajonc (2010) note that in the prevailing scientific dualistic stance of the academy, the education of the whole person as a member of the human collective has been minimized. There is a call for a postreductionistic paradigm that is more aligned with the relational and connected world we live in. Passionate educators care twofold; they are passionate about their discipline and about contributing to the formation of mature and responsible students who will change the world. This work has never been more baffling.

Recent events highlight the deformation of many of our institutional forms. It seems that the daily news publicly questions the integrity of institutions and persons in them. With Facebook's Mark Zuckerberg being

NEW DIRECTIONS FOR TEACHING AND LEARNING • DOI: 10.1002/tl

named *TIME*'s person of the year in 2010, we are reminded of technology's rapidly increasing presence in our society. Will we use it or abuse it? Shirky (2011) suggests anonymity on the Internet may be connected with people behaving badly. Greenfield (2009) worries that students are growing up without a core identity. Work on emerging adulthood (Arnett, 2006) has claimed that the maturity we anticipated in late adolescence emerges in the midtwenties; this suggests students' lived-in experience of college days occurs in tandem with important developmental formation.

Good teaching, more than ever before, includes involvement in the formation of the learner's character and the integration of head and heart. The Circle of Trust® approach offers all educators principles and practices that support this challenging task.

References

Arnett, J. J. "Emerging Adulthood: Understanding the New Way of Coming of Age." In J. J. Arnett and J. L. Tanners (eds.), *Emerging Adults in America: Coming of Age in the 21st Century*. Washington, D.C.: American Psychological Association, 2006.

Aron, L. *A Meeting of Minds: Mutuality in Psychoanalysis*. Hillsdale, N.J.: The Analytic Press, 1996.

Brown, B. The Power of Vulnerability, 2010. Retrieved from http://www.ted.com/speakers/brene_brown.html.

Bussolari, C., and Goodell, J. "Chaos Theory as a Model for Life Transitions Counseling: Nonlinear Dynamics and Life's Changes." *Journal of Counseling and Development*, 2009, 87(1), 98–106.

Diagnostic and Statistical Manual of Mental Disorders IV TR. Washington, D.C.: American Psychological Association, 2000.

Dingfelder, S. F. "Our Stories, Ourselves." *Monitor on Psychology*, 2011, 42(1), 43–45.

Edwards. J. K., and Bess, J. M. "Developing Effectiveness in the Therapeutic Use of Self." *Clinical Social Work Journal*, 1998, 26(1), 89–105.

Fox, J. *Poetic Medicine: The Healing Art of Poem-Making*. New York: Tarcher Putnam, 1997.

Gladding, S. "The Creative Use of Poetry in the Counseling Process." *Personnel and Guidance Journal*, 1979, 2, 285–287.

Goodell, J., and Robinson, D. C. "Through the Glass Darkly: New Paradigms for Counselors, Courage and Spirituality in Contemporary Education." *Catholic Education: A Journal of Inquiry and Practice*, 2008, 11(4). 522–542.

Greenfield, S. *ID: The Quest for Identity in the 21st Century*. London: Sceptre, 2009.

Levitt, H., Butler, M., and Hill, T. "What Clients Find Helpful in Psychotherapy: Developing Principles for Facilitating Moment-to-Moment Change." *Journal of Counseling Psychology*, 2006, 53(3), 314–324.

Lewis, T., Amini, F., and Lannon, R. *A General Theory of Love*. New York: Vintage, 2000.

Luskin, F. *Forgive for Good: A Proven Prescription for Health and Happiness*. New York: HarperCollins Publishers, 2002.

Palmer, P. *The Courage to Teach: Exploring the Inner Landscape of a Teacher's Life*. San Francisco: Jossey-Bass, 1998.

Palmer, P., and Zajonc, A. *The Heart of Higher Education: A Call to Renewal*. San Francisco: Jossey-Bass, 2010.

Seligman, M. *Authentic Happiness*. New York: Free Press, 2002.

Shirky, C. "Cleaning Up Online Conversation." *The HBR Agenda*, 2011, p. 25.

Snyder, C. R., and Lopez, S. J. (eds.). *Handbook of Positive Psychology*. Oxford: Oxford University Press, 2002.

Wampold, B. E. *The Great Psychotherapy Debate*. Mahwah, N.J.: Erlbaum, 2001.

JUDY A. GOODELL, Ed.D., is an associate professor and co-coordinator of the Master's in Counseling Program, marriage and family therapy emphasis, at the University of San Francisco. She is also a licensed marriage and family therapist in private practice and a facilitator for Courage & Renewal programs.

NEW DIRECTIONS FOR TEACHING AND LEARNING • DOI: 10.1002/tl

4

"Found poetry" illustrates how an experimental series of reflective audio teleconference retreats became a transforming experience.

Dialing In to a Circle of Trust: A "Medium" Tech Experiment and Poetic Evaluation

Christine T. Love

A circle of trust is a group of people who know how to sit quietly "in the woods" with each other and wait for the shy soul to show up. The relationships in such a group are not pushy but patient, they are not confrontational but compassionate; they are filled not with expectations and demands but an abiding faith in the reality of the inner teacher and in each person's capacity to learn from it ... The people who help us grow toward true self offer unconditional love, neither judging us to be deficient nor trying to force us to change but accepting us exactly as we are. And yet this unconditional love does not lead us to rest on our laurels. Instead, it surrounds us with a charged force field that makes us want to grow from the inside out—a force field that is safe enough to take the risks and endure the failures that growth requires.

—Palmer, 2004, pp. 59–60

Creating Circles of Trust

In his 2004 book *A Hidden Wholeness*, Parker Palmer makes explicit the unique qualities of the transformational "circle of trust." He describes a group of people embracing the paradox of "being alone together" (p. 54), where the only goal of the group is to invite the emergence of the soul of each individual, through journaling and carefully constructed small and

NEW DIRECTIONS FOR TEACHING AND LEARNING, no. 130, Summer 2012 © Wiley Periodicals, Inc.
Published online in Wiley Online Library (wileyonlinelibrary.com) • DOI: 10.1002/tl.20016

large group work—or simply, through silence (p. 54). Circle of Trust touchstones gently welcome into the circle compassion, a sense of invitation to participate, unconditional love, and faith in each participant's "inner teacher"—all qualities that nurture the "shy soul" to emerge. At the same time, these guiding tenets prohibit behaviors that stunt the growth of soul: communicating expectations or judgment, confrontation, or the "fixing" of others. In these ways, every circle of trust launches an educational journey toward the discovery of each participant's authentic self.

A key tool that participants from teachers to pastors and other serving professionals are taught to carry on this journey is the gently and spaciously paced "honest open question." Palmer (2004) describes it as a "countercultural" invitation to someone who has spoken of a vocational or personal issue to say more "about the matter at hand ... free of the static we create by imposing our own predilections on each other" (p. 130). Honest and open questions are the exact opposite of leading questions: they do not suggest answers or try to fix another who has shared a challenge. Their sole goal is to open rather than restrict the sharer's exploration of his or her concern.

Circles of Trust offer ample opportunity for facilitators to model and teach honest open questions—and for participants to practice this form of questioning that intentionally goes against the grain of advice giving. These questions inform the participants' discussion of how "third things"—typically poems, other short pieces of literature, music, or visual art—intersect with their personal and professional lives. Journaling prompts or suggestions are also typically honest open questions, and participants learn to use their own gentle questions to invite small-group partners into deeper sharing—not to satisfy the asker's curiosity but to serve the answerer's further inner exploration. In clearness committees, the heart of every retreat, the honest open questions of a small group also invite a focus person to think deeply into a concern shared in the strictest confidence. Aimed at supporting the focus person in communicating "with true self, not with other people" (Palmer, 2004, p. 140), honest open questions help a clearness committee "to create and protect a space occupied *only* by the focus person. For the focus person and the committee alike, the questions asked and answers that emerge can be transforming" (p. 144). Another way that circles of trust stand outside of popular cultural norms is that they are the essence of "low tech." Facilitators have historically excluded technology from their circles, wishing to create a more peaceful alternative environment to participants' complex everyday lives. Traditionally circles of trust were also unique *in-person* gatherings experienced by a cohort of professionals convening for a series of seasonal sessions—preferably in retreat settings surrounded by nature. Microphones, laptops, and cell phones were not welcome. Gathering in a simple circle of chairs was not only a signal characteristic of a Circle of Trust, it was originally—and to some, still is—a given that they be convened this way. A number of higher education facilitators made forays into offering Courage to Teach® courses through distance learning (Love, 2010), but for almost two decades most Circle of Trust facilitators literally moved chairs into circles in retreat centers all over the country.

An Experiment Addresses Rural Montana Challenges

Participants from large, rural states like Montana who might wish to take their seats in a Circle of Trust find in this scenario a significant challenge: distance. For some Montanans, experiencing a Circle of Trust retreat means driving up to a thousand-mile round trip. And what low population scattered across wide distances makes challenging, low professional salaries make nearly impossible. These realities were top-of-mind when Montana Courage to Lead® proposed a Courage to Lead for Clergy and Congregational Leaders pilot project in 2008. Several denominations—Disciples of Christ, United Church of Christ, and United Methodist—participated as sponsors from the outset, and the series was eventually opened to leaders of all faiths. With relatively low incomes and minimal staff, many Montana pastors could not afford to attend a traditional seasonal retreat series halfway across the state. At the same time, neither Montana Courage to Lead® nor its denominational partners had access to sophisticated technological support that might support distance learning. Therefore, from the outset, project partners were forced to confront several central questions:

- Could technologically supported retreat experiences successfully supplement an in-person retreat experience to make a series of Circle of Trust opportunities accessible and affordable?
- Could participants build community and develop trust in technologically supported virtual retreat experiences?
- Would participants resist the notion of a "distance retreat"? Would they participate?

   And perhaps most important:

- Could technology be used in a way that would not compromise the transformational learning experience that characterizes the in-person Circle of Trust?

These questions had to be taken into consideration in determining how technology might support a retreat series. Videoconferencing, an obvious high-tech option, was soon discarded because it was too expensive and would still require participants travel to a limited number of videoconference sites. Nor was on-line interface considered optimal, as it did not allow the intimacy of voice connection and required computer access. Skype was eliminated because at the time it could not accommodate up to eight participants. Finally, the Montana project decided on a "medium" tech solution. The plan was to offer pastors an introductory in-person circle of trust followed by a series of four to five monthly audio teleconference book groups, each two hours in length. Cell phones and landlines made this more modest option affordable and accessible to all—for the cost of a long distance call. A free conference call system would provide the bridge.

The planned retreat sequence, gathering in-person first, then by audio teleconference sessions, is supported by both virtual team (Willett, 2002) and on-line learning experience (Lawrence, 1999). Both suggest that initial face-to-face trust building can be critical to the success of a distance group experience. Keeping this wisdom in mind, facilitators convened the first retreat in person and then invited participants to participate in the teleconference series. Participation was voluntary, and forty-three of fifty-nine participants in three separate introductory retreats chose to participate in teleconference retreats. Divided into groups of six to eight, participants were encouraged to read two chapters of Parker J. Palmer's *A Hidden Wholeness* before each monthly session—and to participate in calls even if they had not done the reading. To join a call, each participant dialed a free conference call number set up in advance.

Every effort was made to create a retreat atmosphere during the calls, so in-person retreat practices were followed as closely as possible. A brief silence convened the groups. Then forty-five minutes were devoted to pastor check-ins around a central honest open question, and initial calls included a review of touchstones and honest open questions. Then, as they would in person, participants read a poem or other short selection from one of the assigned chapters for the call. After discussion, the facilitator provided open-ended journal prompts and grouped participants into one of three triads or dyads, each group with a separate call-in number for reconvening after a period of personal journaling. Then all participants hung up and journaled for twenty minutes. Afterward, using different conference call lines, they reconvened in small groups for forty-five minutes. Here, as in the face-to-face retreat, participants one by one shared what they wished from their journals, and their partners offered a few gently paced honest open questions. At the end of small group time, all callers reconvened once more on the original conference call number for a short debriefing on their small-group experiences and setting the next meeting time and chapters assigned. Despite the various on- and off-call steps and numbers involved, participants quickly "got it," and in all various clergy participated in fourteen different sessions following three introductory retreats without a significant hitch.

Orally during the calls and afterward in writing, participants provided feedback and personal anecdotes on the use of technology and retreat practice, and their anonymous responses were collated around the themes that informed the experiment's central questions:

- Participant response to the use of teleconference technology in a retreat series

- Whether participants perceived that a "hybrid" in-person-teleconference retreat series could build the trust and community so essential to Circles of Trust
- Whether participants could experience transformational learning in this mixed learning environment

"Found Poetry" Project Evaluation

Courage & Renewal founding facilitator and research leader Sally Hare encouraged maximum creativity in sharing results of this pilot project. The facilitator selected "pure found poems," a qualitative reporting medium that weaves selected words and phrases from participants' research responses into poetry. Format only is provided by the researcher (hence the "purity" of the format). A key appeal of this medium is that it engages the power of poetry to communicate the essence of participants' affective and behavioral responses to central research questions.

The American Academy of Poets Web site (www.Poets.org) offers the following description of found poems:

> Found poems take existing texts and refashion them, reorder them, and present them as poems. The literary equivalent of a collage ... A pure found poem consists exclusively of outside texts: the words of the poem remain as they were found, with few additions or omissions. Decisions of form, such as where to break a line, are left to the poet.

Monica Prendergast (2009) of Lesley University in Cambridge, Massachusetts, a leader in the use of "poetic inquiry," describes found poetry as a way "to artistically present the work of theorists and or practitioners."

This poetic medium also seemed especially appropriate for reporting on an experiment involving a retreat practice that makes much use of poetry. Further, poetry is increasingly being recognized by the social sciences and humanities as a creative way to both gather and report research results. The found poems that follow share the highlights of participant responses. Most include multiple speakers' words and phrases, whereas a few capture the thoughts of just one person. In all cases, the researcher chose poetic themes and words and crafted poems to reflect accurately the tenor and content of response strands that characterized overall research feedback.

The teleconference call experiment was not without its pitfalls, and three poems illustrate participants' challenges with the design and execution of these calls as a retreat medium. Each expresses an individual view. "Downside" focuses on frustration with small group size and the loss of face-to-face clues to a speaker's feelings, and "Lament" shows the frustration a technical glitch can cause.

Downside

Four people is too many—
not enough silence.

Lack of time
to ask reflective questions.
When the person speaking
may be struggling,
I depend
on body cues.
It would be great
to be in the same room.

Lament

The access code
(wasn't) working.
The technology's hard for me—
always some glitch
that blocks out meaning.

The sole speaker in "Time Together" shows appreciation for the value of the teleconference call sessions but despairs their lack of frequency. In the poignant last lines, the speaker owns the challenge of loneliness.

Time Together

Those
not involved
at all
thought that
there would not
be a lot of value
to these phone calls.
There was
much more value
than I expected.
Once a month
is not frequent enough.
We had just begun to "click"
at the retreat—
but for friendships to develop,
one needs to spend
time together:
They didn't have the opportunity
to grow
in the once-a-month format.

But then, loneliness,
not overwork,
is my main stressor.

"Failure of Logistics" reveals that blending two different teleconference groups during summer when attendance was low had the unintended consequence of shutting down the speaker: the combined group did not feel safe.

Failure of Logistics

Setting up the groups,
you asked
if there was someone
we would rather not be with.
I indicated that there was,
and then,
when the groups were reformed
the last time,
that person was in my group.
It was off-putting:
I did not prioritize
to be part of that session,
and I backed off
in sharing.

I understand
logistics are difficult,
and it probably could not
have been done any other way –
so I should receive it
as a challenge to open up,
but on that day
I was just not able
to do it.

Fortunately, despite heavy initial skepticism, most pastors affirmed that the teleconference experience worked for them as a retreat medium. Four collective poems show that repeating practice from the in-person retreat, as well as the trust developed there, supported achieving deep communication in teleconference—despite participants' original skepticism.

Wednesday Morning

I was really skeptical
about this format.

Leery of
the conference call.
Mixed emotions.
But I'm glad I've come:
Journaling, sharing, listening.
The book and open-ended questions.
The technology did not
interfere.
I am surprised
how much I enjoy it,
how easy to fall back
into retreat:
A basis to build on,
something familiar we have not lost.
I'm grateful for gifts
of communication
and compassion—
a good way to spend Wednesday morning.
This feeds my soul.

Out of the Blizzard

This has worked well
for me
to step out
of the blizzard,
back into retreat:
I know all of you.
What we did
in retreat
makes it easier:
We set the stage
for depth.

Upside

A time of great support,
giving and receiving—
nurturing.
A time for silence
as well as questions.
Time off the phone
to be
with our thoughts.
The sense that I am not alone
in this great big cosmos.
It felt good

to share the heart
of who I am.

Irony

I miss eye contact—
that I do miss.
Visual cues
are so important
that I was kind of
hesitant.
I was surprised
(the calls)
were as effective
as they were.
I was surprised
the phone
could be used to get away.
Wonderful irony
that this little
bane of our existence
could become
a way in(to) retreat.

Another poem, "Over Many Miles That Separate," speaks directly to the depth of spiritual connection that pastors achieved in teleconference.

Over Many Miles That Separate

Good to talk to other pastors—
that seldom happens for me.
Reinforce what was done at the retreat,
continue to work with the concepts in the book.
Personal connection,
insights about myself.
Doing spiritual work with colleagues
at a deeper level than
just politics of the nation,
or the church.
Keep(s) relationships alive
over many miles
that separate me
from others.

During the course of the series, pastors discovered both the power and challenge of using honest open questions, not only among themselves, but also in their relationships with parishioners. "Loving the Questions" articulates both the challenge and wonder they found in this practice.

Loving the Questions

Sometimes it's hard
to ask questions
about feelings
that are open and honest.
to keep the focus
on their concerns—
rather than my curiosity.
I often fall
into the trap
of asking "why?"
and not "how?"
It's hard not to tell
my story.
I have a spotlight image:
It's easy to shift
the spotlight to the listener.
It's like learning a language:
The logic of syntax is reversed.
A lot of this process
is counterintuitive.
I am not resisting:
I love it.

The poem "Before" begins the powerful story a pastor told about using honest open questions to help a suicidal parishioner. She related that one day a member of her congregation called in desperation, telling her, "I don't want to live. I can't fight the system. Everybody hates me." The poem tells the story of what happened before she remembered to stop "fixing" and ask honest open questions.

Before

I had a parishioner
in
suicidal mode:
I was asking
questions,
and when I got
too aggressive,
_____ cried,
"You're not
helping me!"

I reflect on
my past ministry:
I was naturally
curious and aggressive,
and it makes me
want
to cringe.

The pastor, relating the whole story at another time, explained how using honest open questions transformed the call and may have saved her parishioner's life:

At this point I knew I was not in the right place, and I invited _____ to breathe with me. As I sat with _____ in silence over the phone, my training in spiritual direction and honest open questions came back. I realized my spirit was already trying to have a conversation. I needed to get out of my judgmental head. I began to slowly ask _____ honest open questions that invited him to explore what _____ really needed. As I did, the situation on the phone deescalated.

Today _____ is still here. When _____ calls, I just listen ... listen for feelings. Using the new skill caused me to look back on my old way of working with parishioners in crisis...The honest open questions and the whole book [A Hidden Wholeness] really help you get a feel for where you need to be. The most important thing I get out of it is that I can't fix anyone.

Two more collective poems affirmed that the teleconference circle of trust series was transformational for pastors themselves—and that the transformation brought both joy and challenge. "Joy" and "Struggle" describe the two poles of a paradox that may emerge for a pastor who embraces a commitment to authentic self.

Joy

Instead of telling the family answers,
I was more willing to just sit with them.
Instead of feeling like I have to answer their
questions, I make observations
or ask questions to get them
to think more deeply
into
their own questions.
I am not pulling.
It is empowering,
a fascinating process—
applications to many areas

of our lives.
I've tried to balance
boundaries and vulnerability,
not being responsible for the world.
As a pastor, I feel the joy
of seeing us all as equals.
The spirit in you is in us all.
I am looking at giving
my self
more than my skills.
This takes the monkey off my back.

Struggle

My struggle is
to have the courage to lead
as a spiritual leader.
I struggle with
steward leadership.
Since the retreat
I've taken small steps
toward my role as pastor.
I am mindful about inner life
and outer life
and whether they coincide
or not.
A little bit of sadness:
I feel my inner life, if revealed too much,
is not acceptable.
It is also difficult
to rewire and reprogram
our minds and our thinking
to ask open and honest questions,
especially in occupations
routinely expected to have
the answers and the information.

"Occupational Transformation," the voice of a single pastor, and "Paying Attention," a collective poem, amplify pastors' growing awareness that their participation in this teleconference experience has altered both their interaction with peers and their own individual awareness.

Occupational Transformation

I keep myself out:
At a conference,
doing a lot more listening than in the past,

being shaped by this process,
changing the tone,
or helping a conversation
be shaped
in a different way:
Difficult when
working with 16 other folks
using another approach.

Paying Attention

What I am paying
attention to
is what
I clutter my life with
that keeps me
insulated
from my soul.
Paying Attention
What I am paying
attention to
are my responses
as I listen to others—and where
those are coming from.
And to what
people
are really saying,
instead of what
the words
are saying.
I am paying attention
to my need
for solitude,
to expectations.
Grace or love
comes not
when you expect it,
but when you don't.
I am looking for
unexpected
moments
of grace.
and life.

Two final collective poems, "In Need of Circles" and "Resource," affirm that the combined in-person-teleconference retreat experience has initiated very difficult journeys toward personal and professional change for these pastors—and also that they see Circles of Trust as critical sources of support to continue these journeys.

In Need of Circles

Captive to everyone's time.
High expectations
for myself and others.
Not healthy functioning
for myself
and my church.
Guilt that I can't do it all.

Scared
to tell what I need.
Scared
of my own fragility,
to admit I can't do it all.
Scared
of their reaction:
They might reject me
or be angry.

To be exposed, ashamed.
So much of what
people want me to be—
over-functioning—
bad for me and for them.
My inner life,
if revealed, is not acceptable.
Some places where I can risk,
Some places where I can't.

Are some able to claim sole and role?
What is the risk?

Hoping for some place
where I can feel
a sense of community
and belonging,
I am in need of circles
that will help me
go forth with integrity
concerning
vocation.

Resource

In pondering
soul and role,
I have drawn
strength
from the Circle of Trust.
It was helpful
to have
my inner working come out.
It helped
confidence grow in me,
calms me down,
helps me put things in perspective:
Images, phrases
to guide me, to come back to.
When things get
wild and hectic,
the retreat reminds me
to slow down
and center.

This collection of poems answers the questions that informed the Montana Courage to Lead® pilot program for pastors. The poems suggest that, despite challenges, the teleconference medium can support and deepen an in-person retreat experience. They reveal the importance of an initial face-to-face retreat to establish the trust essential to the success of a distance retreat. The poems also illustrate the value of the practice of honest, open-ended questions to pastors' own inner work—and to their practice of their profession. Finally, the poetry suggests that a series of teleconference circles can supplement in-person Circles of Trust in transforming pastors' professional lives.

The success of this experiment led Montana Courage to Lead® and its denominational sponsors to offer a seasonal retreat series: two in-person retreats were held in spring and fall 2011, interspersed with two teleconference retreats in the summer of 2011 and winter of 2012. To round out the series in person, a final in-person gathering will occur in late spring 2012. Thanks to the positive response to the teleconference retreat experience, this mixed medium seasonal series is well underway.

References

Lawrence, R. L. "Cohorts in Cyberspace: Creating Community Online." In Proceedings of the 19th Annual Alliance/ACE Conference, Saratoga Springs, NY, 1999.

Love, C. "The Courage to Use Technology: Circles of Trust Experiments Using High Tech Media." *Words of EnCOURAGEment*, no. 12, [E-Newsletter] Feb. 8, 2010.

Palmer, P. J. *A Hidden Wholeness: The Journey Toward an Undivided Life.* San Francisco: Josssey-Bass, 2004.

Poetic form: found poem. 2011. Retrieved from http://www.poets.org/viewmedia.php /prmMID/5780.

Prendergast, M. "Poetic Inquiry Is ... 29 Ways of Looking at Poetry as Qualitative Research." *Educational Insights,* 2009, *13,* 3.

Willett, C. *What Is a Virtual Team?* Reston, Va.: Applied Knowledge Group, Inc., 2002.

CHRISTINE T. LOVE, M.S.O.D., M.H., facilitates Courage & Renewal retreats for clergy, educators, health professionals, and nonprofit leaders. She also leads Humanities Montana Reflect conversations cosponsored by the national Project on Civic Reflection. She serves as adjunct faculty to the Bitterroot College Program of the University of Montana and currently leads college preparation workshops for nontraditional students. She holds a Master of Science degree from American University and the NTL Institute for Applied Behavioral Science and a Master of Humanities degree from the University of Richmond. Christine completed an undergraduate degree in English at the College of William and Mary.

5

This chapter makes the case for engaging teacher candidates with matters of personal identity and integrity, using explorations of the paradox of self and role, in teacher education programs dominated by a focus on professional knowledge and skills, based on the analysis of interviews with novice teachers.

The Power of Paradox in Learning to Teach

Karen Noordhoff

The preparation of teachers is typically grounded in answers to the question, What knowledge, skills, and dispositions do beginning teachers need to learn and be able to enact (see Darling-Hammond, 2006; Darling-Hammond and Bransford, 2007)? Teacher educators try to help teacher candidates negotiate the significant transition from a focus on themselves as persons becoming teachers to a focus on their students' learning. (See Fuller, 1969, for an early conceptualization of teachers' developmental concerns as they shift from self to students.) Coincidentally, teacher candidates generally think of teacher preparation as learning the tools of the trade, focusing especially on skills such as classroom management and lesson planning. In other words, teacher education usually conceives of teacher preparation as a matter of role adoption or professional development.

Alternatively, another perspective (Danielowicz, 2001; Hansen, 1995; Huebner, 1999; Meijer, Korthagen, and Vasalos, 2009; Palmer, 1998, 2007) sees the process of learning to teach more as identity development or formation and hence, vocation. The root of vocation means "to call," referring to an individual being summoned into service. Hansen (1995) notes that "[t]he sense of vocation finds its expression at the crossroads of public obligation and personal fulfillment. It takes shape through involvement in work that has social meaning and value" (p. 3). Thus, although these scholars and teacher educators do not exclude the need for well-honed teaching skills, they make a significant space for the "person in the profession" (Intrator and Kunzman, 2006, p. 16) in the process of teaching and learning to teach.

NEW DIRECTIONS FOR TEACHING AND LEARNING, no. 130, Summer 2012 © Wiley Periodicals, Inc.
Published online in Wiley Online Library (wileyonlinelibrary.com) • DOI: 10.1002/tl.20017

In this chapter, I argue that both teacher educators and novice teachers (teacher candidates and those in their first year of teaching) can and must engage with personal identity and integrity as those novices learn to take up the professional role of teacher. Including the person in the profession is a good idea because, first, when teacher candidates understand the content and condition of their selfhood, they may recognize their students' selfhood. Second, when novices explore their paths to and passions for teaching, they are invigorated to struggle on behalf of their students under challenging conditions and in times of pressured accountability. Third, as novices negotiate learning to teach in field settings, they may develop autonomy and authenticity while also learning from experienced practitioners. Fourth, learning to hold the paradox of person and profession may help teacher candidates learn to live creatively with ambiguity, a stance that is congruent with the inherent uncertainty of both teaching and learning to teach. (Regarding uncertainties in teaching, see Floden and Clark, 1988; McDonald, 1992.) Finally, novices may begin to build a sustainable life in teaching.

Supporting this argument, I analyze novice teachers' perceptions and experiences of paradox as a means to explore personal identity, or selfhood, and integrity in relation to professional role. In the process, I demonstrate the positive power and feasibility of integrating matters of vocation in teacher education programs. Although I focus on the professional preparation of teachers, this argument and the study on which it is based can readily apply to the education of other professionals, such as counselors, social workers, health professionals, and clergy, in that these roles also require reflection on and learning in ill-defined situations. Too, faculty in the liberal arts and sciences can aid the development of students' capacities to investigate conflicting knowledge claims or multiple, diverse perspectives through their engagement with identity and integrity using the concept of paradox.

Program Context

As a teacher educator in a one-year graduate licensure program, I coordinated two consecutive student cohorts, each with approximately thirty K–8 teacher candidates ranging in age from early twenties through mid-forties. All teacher candidates move as a group through a common curriculum in a sequential set of courses. Cohort leaders may also weave in a special theme usually reflected in a cohort's name—in my cohorts, "Courage to Teach." I integrated a focus on teaching as vocation, specifically the three interrelated concepts of identity, integrity, and paradox from Parker Palmer (1998, 2000, 2007) and the Courage to Teach® program, along with work by Kohl (1984) and Nieto (2003), during two courses I taught across the year, Professional Development and the Reflective Practitioner. Because Palmer (2007) contends *"good teaching cannot be reduced to technique; good teaching comes from the identity and integrity of the teacher"* (italics in the original, p. 10), I engaged the teacher candidates in exploring identity ("self") in the context of teaching and learning to teach ("role"). This paradox, which Palmer (1998, 2007) calls "soul and role," is a significant and compelling arena allowing for the fruitful exploration of a novice's inner life and its relationship to worldly action. However, because I work in a public university where church–state relations matter and because adults can carry negative experiences with religious institutions, I chose to refer to "self and role" in most contexts.

Listen, then, to two teacher candidates from my second cohort, speaking insightfully about their understanding of the relationship of self and role. Kira (all names are pseudonyms) thought of "self as who you really are. … We have a role, but we approach it differently because of who we are." Further, Mi Rae explained "[w]hen I first started the program, I didn't always make that connection that I could be two different roles but still be the same person. Now I realize that I can because I am in the role of being a teacher but I am also me." In these few words, Kira and Mi Rae reference ideas I hoped teacher candidates would take away; they understand that self is more than role and that role does not define selfhood. Further, Kira pointed out that selfhood shapes action within role.

Seeking to understand self and role, we first explored Palmer's (1998) definition of identity, as

> an evolving nexus where all the forces that constitute my life converge in the mystery of self: my genetic makeup, the nature of the man and woman who gave me life, the culture in which I was raised, people who have sustained me and people who have done me harm, the good and ill I have done to others and to myself, the experience of love and suffering—and much, much more. In the midst of that complex field, identity is a moving intersection of the inner and outer forces that make me who I am, converging in the irreducible mystery of being human. (p. 13)

Identity, then, is multifaceted and moving, shaped by apparent opposites—paradoxes such as, "people who have sustained me and people who have done me harm." However, certain aspects can be relatively constant in our mysterious selfhood, such as one's genetics or one's gifts and limits, discussed later.

The second idea we focused upon concerned integrity in which paradox also plays a significant part. By integrity Palmer (1998) means:

> whatever wholeness I am able to find within that nexus as its vectors form and re-form the pattern of my life. Integrity requires that I discern what is integral to my selfhood, what fits and what does not—and that I choose life-giving ways of relating to the forces that converge within me: Do I welcome

them or fear them, embrace them or reject them, move with them or against
them? By choosing integrity, I become more whole, but wholeness does not
mean perfection. It means becoming more real by acknowledging the whole
of who I am. (p. 13)

Here, we learn that integrity involves living in an authentic and generative
way one's full and imperfect identity—successes *and* failures, hopes *and*
despairs, gifts *and* limits. Integrity also implies a connection between who
we are (self) and what we do (role), between inner landscape and worldly
action. This is what I take Palmer (1998, 2007) to mean when he declares,
"we teach who we are" (p. 1).

For example, as one way to reflect on identity and integrity, I asked
teacher candidates to explore the paradoxical relationship of their gifts and
limits. Gifts are not necessarily linked to functions; performance abilities
such as demonstrating organization or writing lesson plans well might better be called talents. (See Jean Vanier on talents and gifts in Muller [1997].)
Rather, gifts are deep ways of being or core qualities characteristic of an
individual's identity, or "self," such as the gift of compassion or discernment. Such a gift is so central to one's being that some version of this quality cannot help but suffuse all the roles a person takes on. The opposite,
but related, side of a gift is a limit. Like two sides of one coin, the gift of
discernment may carry the limit of criticality or insensitivity. Or, a teacher
with the gift of reflection may have difficulty allowing for spontaneity in
her classroom. In other words, striving for integrity as wholeness, a teacher
needs to engage both his gifts and limitations as paradoxical aspects of the
same quality.

Obviously or implicitly, many programs focusing on the obligations
and activities of the teaching role encourage teacher candidates to leave
their selfhood at the door to the university and school classrooms, to live a
life divided between profession and person. However, for children's sakes,
teachers need to bring themselves fully to the classroom. How can a teacher
connect with students in her care, recognize their gifts, help those learners
relate to subject matter, when that teacher is disconnected from her self,
unable to understand her own gifts, to genuinely relate to the world? To
keep heart and to offer themselves in service to their students, teachers
cannot give up their "selves" in servitude; they must hold fast to their identity and integrity while also taking up the obligations of the teaching role—
both for the sake of their students' growth and learning of worthwhile
content and skills.

I turn now to the idea of paradox and the novice teachers' perceptions
of it and experiences with it. I briefly describe the study I conducted,
then present patterns in the novice teachers' perceptions and experiences,
focusing on the paradox of self–role. Finally, I step back to reflect on
what might be learned regarding the professional education of novice
teachers.

NEW DIRECTIONS FOR TEACHING AND LEARNING • DOI: 10.1002/tl

Overview of the Study

Given the integration of ideas about vocation and concepts of identity, integrity, and paradox, which stand in stark contrast to the focus of most teacher education programs, it is useful to understand the sense novices in this program made of these ideas. Specifically, what did the concept of paradox mean to these novice teachers as a way of understanding identity and integrity, in this case from their viewpoints at the end of their first year of teaching? What did they see as its value, if any, for teaching and learning to teach? What paradoxes did they claim to have experienced in the course of the program and during their first year of teaching? How did the paradox of self–role show up in their stories?

One-third ($n = 10$) of the novice teachers who completed the second cohort of the elementary-midlevel preparation program volunteered to be interviewed in the spring of their first year of teaching. The six women ranged in age from their early twenties through mid-thirties (five white, one person of color); three of the four men were in their late twenties, with one in his late thirties (two white, two persons of color). These demographics generally reflect those of the overall cohort, although somewhat more men participated in the study than in the overall cohort (40 percent versus 25 percent, respectively) and the study participants slightly over-represent persons of color compared with the full cohort. However, I make no claim that the experiences and perspectives of the study participants reported here represent the full group.

These first-year teachers spoke with a graduate assistant who had prior experience conducting research interviews; in the case of the present study, she used semistructured questions I prepared. Having a more neutral party engage these novices was important because I had been their cohort leader and an instructor for the program; I wanted them to speak as freely as possible. The audiotaped interviews were transcribed verbatim by a second assistant; I analyzed the data, part of a larger set, using a constant comparative method to develop categories, leading to emergent patterns and themes.

Paradox and Its Meaning for Novice Teachers

In a paradox, two apparent opposites are embraced as one entity, held in tension as a complete and whole truth (Palmer, 2007). Rather than thinking in black and white terms of *either–or*, recognizing or living a paradox requires joining what seems contradictory as *both–and*, within which unity or wholeness can be created. For example, as humans our most direct experience of paradox is in breathing; the act itself is a complete cycle requiring that we *both* breathe in *and* breathe out. We live the paradoxes of solitude *and* community, thinking *and* feeling. Fear and vulnerability are necessary partners to courage and empowerment, respectively. Care of others is not truly possible without care for oneself. In the world of education, obvious paradoxes are teaching *and* learning, theory *and* practice. The poles of these paradoxes may compete for our attention or positive assessment. Yet when held in tension, the connected poles perform like a battery (Palmer), generating the creative energy of life, whereas when they are pulled apart, or we are torn apart by leaning too heavily toward one side or the other, the current stops flowing.

Further, Hole (1999) asks, "Can we exorcise the tension? Should we? What if tension itself is essential to the process of learning for both our students and ourselves? Could I learn to see the tension and discomfort not as a negative thing to be avoided but as a marker, a kind of signpost that says, 'pay attention here, something important is happening'?" (p. 85). As well as helping novices learn to pay attention in life-giving ways to themselves, their students, and their practice, embracing both–and thinking "supports the capacity for connectedness on which good teaching depends" (Palmer, 2007, p. 65). Thus, staying out of either–or thinking can encourage multiple and more imaginative responses to educational dilemmas because how one defines or frames a situation can lead to seeing, or not seeing, particular dimensions and potential responses. Holding onto both poles of a tension may also help teachers see the whole of a child, rather than labeling him as "this way" or "that way."

Meaning and Value of Paradox to Novice Teachers. These novices, speaking from the perspective of a year out from the program and a year into teaching (in regular classrooms, in schoolwide programs, and as substitutes), readily recalled the concept of paradox, appropriately understanding it as a tension or conflict between two opposites. Dawn declared simply that paradoxes are like "comparing opposites," illustrating that teaching is "so much of giving and taking." Leon elaborated paradox as "not one idea or the other idea, but it is both. It is like holding two conflicting things at the same time." Rose got at the complexity of living with paradoxes when she said, "There is no simple black and white way to do something or way to resolve something. ... A lot of paradoxes are never going to go away. You just have to exist in the tension. That is life, it is part of teaching, and it is not a bad thing." Leon and Rose contrasted either–or thinking to both–and thinking as described previously. Rose further astutely noted that many paradoxes are ongoing and, indeed, fundamental to life and work.

Balance. Interestingly, six of the ten novices voluntarily used the commonsense metaphor of "balance" or "balancing" to characterize paradox, terminology not used in the courses. For instance, Miguel commented: "The idea of paradox means trying to strive for balance. ... [T]here is this being stretched maybe or being pulled and then somewhere in the middle you have to find some sort of balance." Describing the relationship of self and role, Genevra actually spoke to the need to "balance the scale," and Samuel did similarly when he stated, "I think it is balancing two different ... opposites and finding that median." Later, he lamented, "[i]n many ways there was a disconnect, so that [the self–role] paradox was more of an imbalance for me." The metaphor of "balance" implies—and some novices here explicitly stated—that there is a midway point or a median, which acts as a stable center.

Value of Paradox. These novices also found the concept of paradox valuable as a support to their teaching and learning to teach, even though they were not directly asked about its worth. Specifically, seven of the ten volunteered three beneficial functions they perceived and experienced. They saw recognizing and living paradoxes as allowing them to name and reflect upon complex situations, create a sense of connectedness between one "self" and one's students, and provide models of being an adult for students.

Some of these novice teachers felt supported in witnessing and understanding the complex and contradictory force fields of their inner and outer lives when using the lens of paradox. Miguel explained, "When I was feeling all these jumbled emotions, it was a way of labeling it, a way of saying 'this is kind of why I am feeling this way.'"

Second, other novices saw the value of holding paradox, particularly in relation to self and role, as doing so created connections between the teacher's selfhood and students. Here, they echo Palmer's point that paradoxes support the capacity for connectedness. Mi Rae, for instance, disclosed that the advice she received from her inner voice is to "know who I am and be who I am and that I am teaching who I am." Continuing, she said, "I think from my experience in student teaching that the times where I tried to be something that I wasn't, it was the hardest part of being a teacher. And the times that I could just, you know, let my true self come out [were] the times when I felt like I really had a sense of community with my students."

Third, Rose noted the power of modeling for students how it is that adults live with paradox, stating, "I think that we can teach children a lot, to see adults dealing with ... seeming conflicts of role, because while we are teaching them fractions and habitats and things like that, we are preparing the next generation of citizens." That Rose framed this value as helping children develop as citizens fits other of her comments, reported later, revealing her democratic ideals.

The remaining three novices—the youngest or least experienced—did not offer any specific benefits of holding and living with paradoxes. Although they initially saw the idea of paradox or its emphasis as "silly" or not very "relevant" during their teacher preparation program, they all concluded by the end of their first year of teaching, in Sydney's words, "Listen to what you're hearing. It may not seem as relevant as it is, but the more you jump into something that is a lot bigger than you can understand at the time, the more you start to understand [about paradoxes]."

Paradoxes Experienced

In this section, I describe the paradoxes these novices named as having occurred during their teacher education program, especially student teaching, and during their first year of teaching, both recalled from their perspectives at the end of that first year. Because the self–role paradox sits at the center of teaching and learning to teach and because I emphasized it throughout the cohort, I was especially curious about the ways that these novice teachers experienced and perceived this tension.

During the Program. Although some of these novice teachers spoke about tensions between roles—for instance, between various family roles and being a teacher in preparation, between being a student and a teacher— seven of the ten novices volunteered examples of the self–role paradox when asked to recall any paradoxes experienced during their teacher education program.

Integral to the self–role paradox and to the context of teaching and learning to teach is the negotiation of authority, a theme that will continue to arise in future examples, as first represented here by Miguel's wondering: "How much do I dictate the direction of the classroom and how much of that is done by the students?" Regarding the power of his own voice, he also wondered how much he should "look to others and let their ideas ... influence what I end up doing." In the latter statement, we might imagine Miguel also considering the influence of his cooperating teacher or the curriculum.

Genevra also explored sources of authority through the self–role paradox. Instead of struggling to give increased voice to the "self" aspect, she seemed to count on the gifts and limits essential to her selfhood while making an effort to embrace the role. An empathetic and compassionate woman, she proclaimed: "Definitely the wanting to be sensitive to students' needs, that is the gift, but then the limit is, or the flip side of that, is being too lenient. ... I tend to get really caught up in self ... so it has been really helpful to realize, yeah, that is important to acknowledge, but also to bring in the role aspect and to look at [my relationships with students] from that viewpoint as well. Both are valid. Both can be held at the same time." She concluded, "Putting on that role actually helped me be more successful in showing who I am"; yet, she also wondered, "When is it more appropriate to bring forth one or the other [to take the lead]?"

Having experienced some classroom management challenges, including one particularly disturbing episode in which a difficult experience from her personal history was reactivated, Genevra realized that she needed to hold the "role" end of the tension along with the "self" pole. She began to think ahead about actions she could take as "teacher" to develop and maintain a positive learning environment, giving credit to "the role and the boundaries that I've put in place to keep everyone successful." By "everyone," I believe she was speaking about herself as well as her students.

Compared to Genevra's life-giving connection between the polarities of self and role, Samuel spoke to a disheartening disconnection between his identity as a caring male and military veteran and his teaching role. He contrasted what he perceived as "acceptable or required in the classroom versus my experience, my past and what I had been through. In many ways there was a disconnect, so that paradox was more of an imbalance for me." In his particular upper elementary student teaching setting, Samuel felt he had to justify his capacity to be a nurturing male. Then again, he also felt he could not talk about what he had learned from his war experience, although he realized raising such matters needed to be appropriate to his students. Samuel thought this situation resulted from working in a some-what conservative setting requiring him to be "politically correct," ulti-mately a context that he felt sapped the authority of his identity.

During the First Year of Teaching. All but one novice identified par-adoxes occurring during their first year of teaching in relation to author-ity—with students in the classroom, at the school level with teaching col-leagues, and with parents. Following are several striking illustrations, emphasizing instances of the self–role paradox.

Leon described what he saw as "one of the key paradoxes [in] being a teacher … this balance of creating a relationship with your kids, like get-ting to know them and letting them get to know you openly so they see you are a person and value you. But there is a fine line. … So it is like you want to have that bond, but at the same time still hold the authority in the class-room and make sure you are still respected. … That is a tough one." Although this tension is not new to preservice or practicing teachers, nota-bly Leon framed it as a paradox, although without the language of both–and ("you want to have that bond, but at the same time still have the author-ity"). Doing so potentially helped Leon see ways to maintain connections and authority, rather than feeling that getting to know kids and them, him, just does not work.

Rose found that "there is no inherent conflict between me being myself and being a good teacher," something that surprised her, and in fact, the key to being a good teacher is being oneself. "When who I am and how I want to do things, and things that interest me, come into conflict with cur-riculum, I [figure] out how to put it all together. … Some of the specific things that are not [in the] curriculum that I teach them about are [setting personal and academic] goals, respecting your voice, valuing voice. … I guess it is an example of the values that I have that I brought into the room that are not specifically part of our curriculum." In other words, she taught students "to value who they are and value one another and their differ-ences." In these comments and others, Rose described adding to the planned curriculum by enacting a collective classroom climate valuing inclusion of diverse voices and individual responsibility. Not merely a mat-ter of "classroom procedures" (as she says elsewhere), she conveyed a meaningful curricular dimension consistent with democratic values.

She concluded, "I mean the more comfortable [a teacher is] in their skin, I think the smoother the class goes and the more the kids learn." Thus, Rose believed that teachers living with integrity (being "comfortable in their skin") leads to more learning by students. Moreover, her clarity conveys a firm sense of her identity and integrity, her examples providing obvious and authentic connections between what she values and her actions as a teacher. For a novice teacher who the year before had characterized herself as feeling like an elephant in a tutu, Rose helps us picture a novice at ease in her own authority.

Tragic Gap. Given their perceptions of schools, two male novices found it especially difficult to integrate their identities into their teaching. In particular, they struggled with what they called the "realities" of schools in contrast to the "ideals" taught in their teacher education program. Aiden proclaimed clearly: "The paradox number one is what you are taught at grad school and what it is like in a school." Similarly, Samuel pointedly remarked, "The world of the teaching preparation program versus the world of the actual classroom is somewhat different. ... It is just possibly lacking the connection to what the classroom really is presently versus the ideal." Recall, too, Samuel's remarks earlier about disconnection, imbalance, and the character of the collegial environment in which he worked as a student teacher. These novices spoke with frustration, even despair, about the tension between what is (reality) and what can be (possibility), a paradox Palmer (2009) has termed a "tragic gap" (p. 175)—tragic in the ancient Greek sense that the space between the two poles is inevitable and ongoing.

Whereas Leon's, Genevra's, and Rose's previous commentaries about negotiating the self–role paradox give a sense of wholeness, even as they experienced challenges, Aiden and Samuel described seemingly acute inner conflict attempting to live their identities in the realities they perceived in schools. Perhaps they were living lives divided between the personal and the professional. Aiden's comments are especially articulate and ultimately poignant: "[I]t would be hard for me if I just went into school every day and focused on a role that I was supposed to play. ... I would feel just sterile and it would feel very disconnected, and it wouldn't feel like human beings in a room together, teaching each other and learning from each other. Yeah, if I don't bring who I am to class, I don't even know if I could do it, personally. I don't know if I can teach in a disconnected fashion." These deep sentiments could make for a tension difficult to manage in combination with Aiden's sense of the disheartening realities of schools. I believe Aiden left teaching after his third year.

I offer these words from Aiden and Samuel not to discourage readers (or myself) but to keep in front of us the overall complexity of identity and integrity work, as well as its individual intricacies. At the same time, their stories give a more inclusive sense of the perspectives of the novices interviewed for this study.

NEW DIRECTIONS FOR TEACHING AND LEARNING • DOI: 10.1002/tl

The Power of Paradox in Teacher Education

In this chapter, I have argued and demonstrated that both teacher educators and novice teachers can and need to engage with personal identity and integrity as those novices learn to take up the role of "teacher." I have demonstrated that developing novices' capacities to hold paradoxes, such as gifts–limits and, particularly, self–role, is one fruitful opportunity within teacher preparation programs to help novices understand themselves and their roles, how to "teach who we are" in a sustainable and appropriate way.

From their perspectives at the end of the first year of teaching, the ten novices who participated in the reported study recalled, understood, and valued the concept of paradox during both teacher preparation and first-year teaching. Many additionally described paradox through the metaphor of "balance." Balance may not always imply a static state but rather an ongoing movement toward a shifting equilibrium. Still, I wonder whether or not living with paradox as a "balancing" act fosters the capacity to generate new ways of being or acting from creatively living the tension of apparent opposites. If not, perhaps I needed to be more explicit helping novices to grasp and use this concept more deeply and imaginatively. Perhaps, as well, novice teachers' varying understandings and uses of paradox may situate them along a continuum of appreciation and action in relation to the concept.

Briefly, my second wondering regarding these novices' understanding of paradox concerns *both–and* thinking in relation to adult development. I wonder whether younger or less experienced novices relate to the idea of paradox as readily as older and more experienced novices may. However, I am skeptical of developmental theories when misinterpreted to imply that without having reached a particular level or stage, one cannot engage with a particular life task or concept. That even the younger, less experienced novices here came to understand and value paradox points to its potential to help them learn to hold self and role together.

Overall, the use of paradox as a lens to understand and live more fully into identity and integrity helped the novices reflect on, make sense of, and negotiate their selfhood, their teaching practice, and the relationship between the two. They used paradox to look at their feelings and attitudes and mind-sets, relationships with students and other teachers, as well as consideration and creation of learning environments. Matters of authority and authenticity permeated these novices' experiences and perceptions, a claim that may not surprise teacher educators who regularly deal with beginning teachers and classroom management. Yet the perspectives described by these novice teachers seem significantly different from the typical emphasis on classroom authority concerned with rules and respect derived from strategies of classroom organization and discipline. Rather, their engagement with the self–role paradox put the emphasis on seeking and acting from an authentic ground of their being, in addition to technique. In other words, through paradox these novices sought to author their own lives at the vocational intersection where one's "deep gladness [or selfhood] meets the world's deep need" (Buechner, 1993, p. 119).

Let me be clear that I do not claim that teaching solely from one's selfhood is sufficient in today's schools; I have been a teacher and teacher educator for enough decades to know that well-honed skills do make a difference. But I do claim that without a teacher's deep sense of his or her own identity, expressed authentically through integrity, teaching skill is not sufficient to truly connect with learners and help them connect with worthwhile subject matter and to themselves.

So, I ask my university colleagues and myself: How might our teacher education and other professional programs embody the paradox of *both* identity and integrity *and* appropriate professional knowledge, skills, and dispositions within our curricula and pedagogies? How can we engage and develop the person in the profession at the same time we develop conceptual frameworks and technical skills? Perhaps this chapter gives a glimpse of the powerful possibilities. Perhaps we can further support novices like Aiden and Samuel, as well as their cohort colleagues, to create sustainable lives as teachers. Perhaps we can help our novices learn to live teaching lives full of passion—with both its suffering *and* its joys.

References

Buechner, F. *Wishful Thinking: A Seeker's ABC.* San Francisco: HarperSanFrancisco, 1993.

Danielowicz, J. *Teaching Selves: Identity, Pedagogy, and Teacher Education.* Albany: State University of New York, 2001.

Darling-Hammond, L. *Powerful Teacher Education: Lessons from Exemplary Programs.* San Francisco: Jossey-Bass, 2006.

Darling-Hammond, L., and Bransford, J. (eds.). *Preparing Teachers for a Changing World: What Teachers Should Learn and Be Able to Do.* San Francisco: Jossey-Bass, 2007.

Floden, R., and Clark, C. M. "Preparing Teachers for Uncertainty." *Teachers College Record,* 1988, 89(4), 505–524.

Fuller, F. F. "Concerns of Teachers: A Developmental Conceptualization." *American Educational Research Journal,* 1969, 6(2), 207–226.

Hansen, D. T. *The Call to Teach.* New York: Teachers College Press, 1995.

Hole, S. "Teacher as Rain Dancer." In E. Mintz and J. T. Yun (eds.), *The Complex World of Teaching: Perspectives from Theory and Practice.* Cambridge, Mass.: Harvard Educational Press, 1999.

Huebner, D. "Teaching as Vocation." In V. Hillis (ed.), *The Lure of the Transcendent: Collected Essays by Dwayne E. Huebner.* Mahwah, N.J.: Lawrence Erlbaum Associates, Inc., 1999.

Intrator, S. M., and Kunzman, R. "The Person in the Profession: Renewing Teacher Vitality through Professional Development." *Educational Forum,* 2006, 71(1), 16–32.

Kohl, H. *Growing Minds: On Becoming a Teacher.* New York: Harper and Row, 1984.

McDonald, J. P. *Teaching: Making Sense of an Uncertain Craft.* New York: Teachers College Press, 1992.

Meijer, P. C., Korthagen, F.A.J., and Vasalos, A. "Supporting Presence in Teacher Education: The Connection Between the Personal and Professional Aspects of Teaching." *Teaching and Teacher Education*, 2009, 25(2), 297–308.

Muller, W. *How Then Shall We Live? Four Simple Questions that Reveal the Beauty and Meaning of Our Lives.* New York: Bantam Books, 1997.

Nieto, S. *What Keeps Teachers Going?* New York: Teachers College Press, 2003.

Palmer, P. J. *The Courage to Teach: Exploring the Inner Landscape of a Teacher's Life.* San Francisco: Jossey-Bass, 1998.

Palmer, P. J. *Let Your Life Speak: Listening for the Voice of Vocation.* San Francisco: Jossey-Bass, 2000.

Palmer, P. J. *The Courage to Teach: Exploring the Inner Landscape of a Teacher's Life.* 10th Anniversary Ed. San Francisco: Jossey-Bass, 2007.

Palmer, P. J. (2009). *A Hidden Wholeness: The Journey Toward an Undivided Life.* San Francisco: Jossey-Bass, 2009.

KAREN NOORDHOFF *is a teacher educator at Portland State University and a facilitator of Circles of Trust (including Courage to Teach®) programs for 12 years. She thanks the PSU Faculty Development Fund for support of this research.*

6

This chapter investigates the role of identity in teaching and learning. The chapter draws connections between the process of transformational education and the practice of leadership.

The Role of Identity in Transformational Learning, Teaching, and Leading

Michael I. Poutiatine, Dennis A. Conners

In professional practice contexts, the technical questions (Heifetz, 1994; Heifetz, Linksy, and Glasgow, 2009) are rarely the ones that prove most difficult. Rather, the real questions that arise from complex and ambiguous contexts, and that require learners, teachers, and leaders to examine deeply held beliefs about selfhood, integrity, ethics, and justice, often prove to be the most challenging. The lesson for leadership is that the real world is messy and requires that we attend to wholes, not just parts. As we engage in the practice of teaching, learning, and leading in the real world, such a stance requires having the right kind of eyes to see these thorny situations for what they truly are. Some contend that this kind of perspective is largely a matter of natural disposition, but we contend that this kind of vision can be developed. A recent role-playing simulation in a graduate leadership preparation program demonstrates the tensions between identity and integrity, as well as the pedagogical implications of examining such tensions. In the following example, we can begin to see the complex dance of formation and transformation that is required if we are to develop our capacities for teaching, learning, and leading.

The Classroom Simulation

A student of educational leadership becomes a first-year principal and arrives at school for her first day of work. She is a bright-eyed educator

NEW DIRECTIONS FOR TEACHING AND LEARNING, no. 130, Summer 2012 © Wiley Periodicals, Inc.
Published online in Wiley Online Library (wileyonlinelibrary.com) • DOI: 10.1002/tl.20018

who has a deep conviction about leading for educational excellence for all children. Her first meeting is with an illegal immigrant Mexican mother who wants to register her elementary-aged children for school. The mother speaks only Spanish; the principal hastily finds a translator. The mother has asked to meet the principal because she has heard that this is a good school and she wants the best for her children.

The School. The principal's simulated school resides in a state that recently passed a law forbidding districts from spending money to educate illegal immigrants. The law was contested in the courts but currently stands. The district's board approved a policy implementing the law, and the district administration directed every principal to verify the legal status of all students as well as to use a new and intrusive registration form.

The Conversation. The principal begins by engaging the parent, but as the conversation unfolds, the principal falters as the mother pleads with her, explaining that she has come to this school so that her children "can have a better life." The mother worries that she will be reported to the Immigration and Naturalization Service if she fills out the form, yet she knows that school is the only avenue by which her children can move forward.

The Question. The novice principal immediately faces a question common to school leaders: What do I believe about my identity as an educator, and what does my job require of me right now? Or, more simply stated, who am I and how do I manifest that with integrity in the moment? In the context of the simulation, an intellectual exercise becomes a dunking in the messy reality of personal identity, practical integrity, and the practice of leadership. Neither the principal candidate nor the observing cohort can escape the exercise without beginning to recognize their own capacities to do harm in the service of their schools—harm to others and harm to themselves through the deformation of their identities. The tension created by standing in the "tragic gap" (Palmer, 2004) between identity and integrity is palpable in the room. Further, the students begin to see that if we as educational leaders want to engage in the work of transforming students, organizations, and systems toward a more just and ethical practice, we must be very clear about the role our own identities play in our practice of teaching, learning, and leading.

We believe that the most challenging work of preparing learners, teachers, and leaders is discerning the answers to these questions: How do I lead from my beliefs when my job or life seems to require something outside of or counter to those beliefs? How do I align my internal identity with my external integrity? Or, simply, what do I do when I don't know what to do? This chapter suggests a conceptual framework supporting the argument that in order for teachers and educational leaders to engage with the world on both practical and idealistic levels, a formational and transformational developmental approach is necessary.

Formation and Transformation

Amid the often seemingly impersonal bureaucracy of educational practice, we occasionally find that elegant question that frames our thought for years to come. As coauthors and colleagues, we found that this elegant "question" moment came for us while having lunch outside on a warm summer day when the seemingly innocent question of "What is the difference between formation and transformation?" was posed. We have slowly fallen in love with this question. It is this question that we think is most salient to a deeper life of teaching, learning, and leading in ways that can transform our world in the service of social justice. And, in our simulation case, it is the question that was at the heart of that exercise.

During our exploration of the ideas of Parker Palmer (Intrator and Kunzman, 2006; Palmer 1983/1993, 1998a, 1998b, 2000, 2004), we looked carefully at the Courage to Teach® retreat model that Palmer and the Center for Teacher Formation (now Center for Courage & Renewal) have created for teachers and educational leaders. These retreats are designed to engage educators with identity formation processes and to offer safe space for honoring their souls. The retreats generally take place seasonally and in quiet, hospitable places (Poutiatine, 2005). The formational approach of these retreats is one of exploring the inner landscape of beliefs and values and connecting them with what we do as people. Participants are offered many ways to engage with this work in a deeply invitational way. In one study (Poutiatine, 2005), we found that the participants in Courage to Teach® or Courage to Lead® retreats tended to engage with the retreat in one or more of four modes: (1) as retreat or respite; (2) as identity formation; (3) as identity and integrity formation; and (4) as the seed for transformational process. In Poutiatine's 2005 work on understanding these four modes, the relationship between formation and transformation was found to take on a developmental meaning for educators and educational leaders.

Formation as Retreat. In this mode of engagement, participants often came to the retreat process simply to recharge (Poutiatine, 2005). The participants tended to look at these retreats as a place to get away from the daily grind—places to eat some good food and to have meaningful conversation with lovely people in a quiet and caring space.

Formation as Engagement with Identity. In this mode of engagement, Poutiatine (2005) found that some retreat participants came to remember (Palmer, 1998a, p. 30) who they were. This way of being in formation retreats often led participants to reconnect with who they are, with their core ideals, ideas, and values. This process is formational in nature, as it helps us move into clarity about our being and place in the world. As stated by Palmer (Fetzer Institute, 1999), "Formation means the creation of trustworthy and evocative spaces where the human soul can do exactly that, regain its original form."

Formation as Engagement with Integrity. In this mode of engagement retreat, participants spoke not only of allowing their identity or soul to regain its original form but also about being clear regarding how that form is to be manifest in the world (Poutiatine, 2005). Such a manifestation represents an integration of not only who a person is but also of what he or she does in the world and of how those two things can be made more congruent. This mode of engagement, however, still does not imply a fundamental reformation of the identity, but only a recommitment to the implied integrity of that identity.

Formation as the Seed of Transformation. There was a contingent who described the experience of engaging in formation retreats as transformational (Poutiatine, 2005). These participants found that the process consisted of more than getting reacquainted with identity or finding ways to better manifest that identity. For them, the experience was about recreating, rebuilding, their integrity based on their emergent understandings of identity. This process was transformational rather than formational in that a process of fundamental change was at work. Rather than becoming more of themselves, these participants articulated an experience of becoming fundamentally different as a result of deep engagement with their own identity and integrity. From their perspective, a new person emerged.

It is interesting to note that initially, the majority of participants in this study (Poutiatine, 2005) came to teacher formation retreats for one of the first three modes of engagement, but not for transformation. Thus, formation and transformation can be differentiated through the idea that formation primarily involves a reconnection with one's existent core identity, whereas transformation involves the reformation of that core identity. From this perspective, the fundamental work of transformation must begin with formational work. However, to understand this notion in the context of the individual or the organization, the nature of the transformative process that can be triggered through formational work (Poutiatine, 2005) must be explored.

The Simulation Revisited

After our young principal's simulation experience, we held a lengthy debriefing with the cohort. During this debriefing, the principal candidate articulated clearly the inner turmoil that this experience incited. For her, the experience of facing the formational question of identity and integrity in practice was the seed of her transformative journey. She realized in that moment that who she was as an educator would not be adequate to do the job she wanted to do and that a recreation of that identity was required. This candidate returned repeatedly to the moment when, speaking to a young mother about the future of her children, she saw the real work of school leadership: aligning who she was with what she was doing. In the words of this candidate, "That moment changed my life."

The Nature of Transformative Process

Humans have always recognized the power of transformational change, and such change has always been a source of wonder for us. Legends regarding the process of transformation can be traced to some of the earliest myths of human civilization (Campbell, 1949). The mysterious process of becoming more than we thought we could has been studied across many disciplines. Particularly cogent and articulate explorations of transformational process have come from Patricia Cranton (1994, 1996) and Jack Mezirow (1990, 1997; Mezirow and Associates, 2000).

Transformative Learning Theory. Both Cranton (1996) and Mezirow (1991) suggest that humans construct worldviews or meaning schemes in order to make sense of the world and to provide a framework for personal and collective agency. Meaning schemes are based upon experiences that can be deconstructed and acted upon in a rational way (Taylor, 1998). Mezirow (1991) suggests that this happens through a series of phases that begins with the disorienting dilemma—that is, the experience or informational awareness that is not congruent with the person's existing meaning schema or worldview.

As Cranton (1996) and Mezirow (1990) suggest, the disorienting dilemma can be a cognitive process; or, as Dirkx (2006) suggests, a process engaged through other ways of knowing. In any case, the disorienting dilemma represents a seed of a new consciousness that can be either explored or ignored. The choice to explore this consciousness and to eventually integrate it into the worldview is the process of transformation. This process has a consistent and recognizable pattern that always starts with a shift in consciousness. As noted earlier, the process of formation can generate the disorienting dilemma (Poutiatine, 2005) that is the seed of transformation, but does not necessarily do so. Transformative process can also be considered developmental as a cyclical process of identity formation and reformation.

For our young aspiring principal, that disorienting dilemma was rooted in the formational process of identity and integrity: the dilemma of who we are and what we do. She found her disorienting dilemma in the formational question, How do I act in alignment with what I believe when I am called by the system in which I am embedded to act differently? Her call to transformation came as a result of a formational process triggered by a technical situation. It is interesting to note that this principal candidate could have chosen to ignore the call that this dilemma of practice created; she could have simply adhered to the "letter of the law" and forgotten it, but she could not do that. Instead, she chose to engage in a process of reforming her identity and her practice with greater integrity, to emerge as a new practitioner. This choice opened a path for the educator that took her many months to complete, but she continues to this day to note the instant when she made the choice, the moment when she really decided to become a leader for schools and for justice. The implications flowing from this case can lead us to look more deeply not only at the practice of preparing educational leaders, but also at the practice of facilitating growth in professional practitioners in many fields. This brings us to the work of Robert Kegan (1982, 1994; Kegan and Lahey, 2001, 2009).

Robert Kegan and Transformative Development. Robert Kegan, a constructive-developmental psychologist, offers us a different framework for looking at both formation and transformation. Kegan (1982, 1994) suggests that the constantly changing demands of modern life may be developmentally inappropriate for many, perhaps even most, adults. He explains, "The expectations upon us ... demand something more than mere behavior ... or the mastery of particular knowledge. They make demands on our minds, on *how* we know, on the complexity of our consciousness" (Kegan, 1994, p. 5). Kegan's theory relies on several premises, the primary one being that the systems by which people make meaning grow and change over time and that this growth takes place via radical shifts of worldview—transformations. He makes a clear distinction between information and transformation, pointing to information as new knowledge that one adds to the current *form* of one's mind and that, although helpful, is generally by itself not a sufficient kind of growth for adults. Kegan's informational learning or growth, then, is more about creating or developing a larger, deeper, and more effective connection with what one already has (the current form of mind, be that objective knowledge or subjective self-knowledge) rather than being about reforming the relationship with that objective or subjective knowledge base.

Transformation, by contrast, is about changing the very *form* of the container—remaking it larger, more complex, more able to deal with multiple demands and uncertainties. Kegan (1994) observes that transformative learning happens when someone changes "not just the way he behaves, not just the way he feels, but the way he knows—not just what he knows but the *way* he knows" (p. 17). According to Kegan, transformation must encompass not just a formational development of the self (mind, heart, spirit, and so on) but also an actual remaking of that self and the very way in which the self knows the world. For Kegan, this transformational remaking of self always requires an increasing differentiation and internalization of the relationship between self and other.

This shift in consciousness regarding self and other can be seen as characteristic of the formation and transformational learning paradigms. In order for any real transformation to take place, a deep and broad understanding of the self and how it is manifest in the world is required. The transformational shift in consciousness that Kegan (1994) describes is predicated on a formational connection with the selfhood. If the principal in our opening example is not clearly connected with her own selfhood and with the beliefs, mission, goals, and behaviors associated with that identity, then remaking that identity through reconstructing relationships with Kegan's (1982) "other" will not be possible. In short, for Kegan, transformation is dependent on formation. If this is true, then Kegan's ideas have implications for both teaching and leading for transformation.

Teaching and Leading for Transformation

As most theory of transformational learning indicates, transformation always is a personal process (Schlitz, Vieten, and Amorok, 2007). It may be triggered by events inside or outside the person, but the actual process is one of identity formation and reformation (Kegan, 1982, 1994; Palmer, 1998a, 2004). This is to say that if I am called to a shift in consciousness, this shift must be in part about my identity, as my identity construct is always integral to my worldview. As I am part of the world, my consciousness of the world must always be framed by my consciousness of myself. This is the basis of the common statement of transformational experience: "I am a completely different person now than I was before [transformational experience]." The transformational experience forms and reforms my identity and must, by definition. If this is so, then the process of teaching and leading for transformation must be an intentional one that is grounded in identity, both of the teacher or leader and the led.

The Principal's Dilemma Again. Potential for transformational learning on the part of our young principal becomes apparent here. In the simulation, she is faced with the superficial transactional decision of forcing the illegal immigrant parent to register and potentially face deportation or not forcing this issue. This seemingly simple technical decision creates in her the need to hold the tensions created by her own identity as an educator. She is deeply conflicted in holding the tension between her beliefs and the demands of the system within which she works. On an even deeper level, however, she is faced with the invitation to transform herself through connection with her own identity and how she chooses to manifest that identity with integrity in the present context. Her previous identity construct offers her an either/or dilemma with no clear way forward. In order to proceed with integrity, a degree of wholeness, her call is to remake her identity so that it is congruent with a holism that she recognizes to be absent in the moment. Her current formational connection with her beliefs is not enough. In this moment she is called to, as Kegan (1994) puts it, "change the way [s]he knows" herself and the world, and perhaps with new eyes she can see that change in the systems she inhabits. This, then, is the fulcrum of leadership for a purpose greater than ourselves: to make the choice not only to transform ourselves but also to be an agent in transforming the very systems in which we operate, based on the integrity of our own souls and the integrity of those whom we serve.

Conclusion

Our novice principal's case illustrates the mental demands that the work of real leadership places on individuals. It is the process of developing a formational relationship with the self and the need to exercise transformational developmental capacities in order to be successful (Kegan, 1994). This chapter argues that we can be intentional about teaching and leading for these processes. An intention grounded in formational and transformational concepts can effect developmental changes in participants' behaviors and beliefs. These changes are critically important because individuals often are unaware of how their underlying assumptions affect their actions. If we are to effectively develop teachers, learners, and leaders who can hold the tensions found in the tragic gap between the real and the ideal (Palmer, 2004), we must start with formation and transformational process.

Designing approaches and programs that have these types of significant effects on participants' minds and beliefs is complex, as we must work to challenge participants' fundamental assumptions about how they think about and do their work. This challenge is new to the field, because "much of what goes under the banner of professional development amounts to helping us develop more skills or capacities to cope, but to cope within the worlds of our assumptive designs. The design itself is never in question" (Kegan and Lahey, 2001, p. 71). We echo Kegan and Lahey's critique of professional development and extend it to include the variety of ways in which adults are taught or credentialed. Although individuals often are resistant to changing their conceptions about their work, the most powerful programs will address and challenge these limiting beliefs and assumptions, thereby helping participants to acquire new ones that are aligned not only with skills and knowledge, but also with a clear grounding in the beliefs and identity of the learner, teacher, and leader (Poutiatine and Conners, 2012). If the effectiveness of learning, teaching, and leadership is always predicated on the internal state of the person, the work of formation, we must address that work in our developmental work as teachers, learners, and leaders. Further, we must understand the process of transforming that internal state to achieve more effective practice.

References

Campbell, J. *The Hero With a Thousand Faces.* Princeton, N. J.: Princeton University Press, 1949.

Cranton, P. *Understanding and Promoting Transformative Learning: A Guide for Educators of Adults.* San Francisco: Jossey-Bass, 1994.

Cranton, P. *Professional Development as Transformative Learning: New Perspectives on Teachers of Adults.* San Francisco: Jossey-Bass, 1996.

Dirkx, J. "Authenticity and Imagination." In P. Cranton (ed.), *Authenticity in Teaching.* New Directions for Adult and Continuing Education, no. 111. San Francisco: Jossey-Bass, 2006. doi:10.1002/ace.225

Fetzer Institute. "Teaching from the Heart: Seasons of Renewal in a Teacher's Life." Video Recording. Kalamazoo, Mich.: Fetzer Institute, 1999.

Heifetz, R. *Leadership without Easy Answers*. Cambridge, Mass.: Harvard University Press, 1994.

Heifetz, R., Linsky, M., and Glasgow, A. *The Practice of Adaptive Leadership*. Boston: Harvard Business Press, 2009.

Intrator, S., and Kunzman, R. "The Person in the Profession: Renewing Teacher Vitality through Professional Development." *Educational Forum*, 2006, 71, 16–32.

Kegan, R. *The Evolving Self*. Boston: Harvard University Press, 1982.

Kegan, R. *In Over Our Heads: The Mental Demands of Modern Life*. Cambridge, Mass.: Harvard University Press, 1994

Kegan, R., and Lahey, L. L. *How the Way We Talk Can Change the Way We Work: Seven Languages for Transformation*. San Francisco: Jossey-Bass, 2001.

Kegan, R., and Lahey, L. *Immunity to Change*. Boston: Harvard Business Press, 2009.

Mezirow, J. *Fostering Critical Reflection in Adulthood*. San Francisco: Jossey-Bass, 1990.

Mezirow, J. *Transformational Dimensions of Adult Learning*. San Francisco: Jossey-Bass, 1991.

Mezirow, J. "Transformative Learning: Theory to Practice." In P. Cranton (ed.), *Transformative Learning in Action: Insights from Practice*. New Directions for Adult and Continuing Education, no. 74. San Francisco: Jossey-Bass, 1997.

Mezirow, J., and Associates. *Learning as Transformation*. San Francisco: Jossey-Bass, 2000.

Palmer, P. J. *To Know as We Are Known*. New York: HarperOne, 1983/1993.

Palmer, P. J. *The Courage to Teach*. San Francisco: Jossey-Bass, 1998a.

Palmer, P. J. "Leading from Within." In L. Spears (ed.), *Insights on Leadership* (pp. 197–208). New York: John Wiley & Sons, 1998b.

Palmer, P. J. *Let Your Life Speak*. San Francisco: Jossey-Bass, 2000.

Palmer, P. J. *A Hidden Wholeness: The Journey Toward an Undivided Life*. San Francisco: Jossey-Bass, 2004.

Poutiatine, M. I. "The Role of Identity and Integrity in Teacher Development: Towards a Grounded Theory of Teacher Formation." Unpublished doctoral dissertation, Gonzaga University, 2005.

Poutiatine, M. I., and Conners, D. A. "Teaching Leadership for Socially Just Schools: A Transformational Approach." In J. Barbour and G. Hickman (eds.), *Leadership for Transformation*. San Francisco: Jossey-Bass, 2012.

Schlitz, M., Vieten, C., and Amorok, T. *Living Deeply: The Art and Science of Transformation in Everyday Life*. Oakland, Calif.: New Harbinger, 2007.

Taylor, E. W. *The Theory and Practice of Transformative Learning: A Critical Review*. 1998. Columbus: ERIC Clearinghouse on Adult, Career, and Vocational Education, Ohio State University. (ED 423 422)

MICHAEL I. POUTIATINE *is an adjunct instructor of leadership studies at Gonzaga University in Spokane, Washington.*

DENNIS A. CONNERS *is an associate professor of leadership studies at Gonzaga University in Spokane, Washington.*

7

This chapter describes a model program for transformative professional development, which may contribute to greater trust, beneficial self-reflection, and community transformation for educators.

Lessons Learned from Transformational Professional Development

Twyla T. Miranda

"I never knew that was how my principal felt."

"I learned more about myself and how I respond as a teacher. I've learned that the creativity I expressed as a child is part of who I am."

"I now have a group I can go to with a problem—or a celebration, and with a level of extreme trust."

"I feel renewed and ready to 'go with the flow'—I'm actually excited about this new school year."

These were comments made by teachers and school leaders as we concluded our fifth Transformative Professional Development retreat together. Meeting together in retreats over a school year had provided valuable opportunities for critical reflection, validation, and development of trust with colleagues. Assumptions about experiences and perceptions as educators were considered, discussed, and often reorganized into new definitions. Such revisiting and revisioning resonate with transformative learning theory (Cranton, 1994; Kitchenham, 2008; Mezirow, 1991; Scott, 1997) and with the belief that teachers and school leaders respond favorably to invitational, planned, safe space for professional development. One component of transformative learning theory is that adults "develop a conviction that meaning exists within ourselves rather than in external forms such as books and that personal meanings that we attribute to our experience are acquired and validated through human interaction and communication" (Mezirow, 1991, p. xiv).

What is transformative professional development for educators? Ideally, teachers and school leaders are given multiple opportunities to revisit schemas about themselves and their learning communities, with the intent to transform practice, the school environment, and even themselves (Jurow, 2009). In practice, our three cohorts of teachers and school leaders completed a yearlong program of professional development retreats, offered seasonally and funded entirely by two external partners, the Fetzer Institute of Kalamazoo, Michigan, and Texas Wesleyan University, Fort Worth, Texas. Teachers and school leaders were invited to spend both quality and quantity time in order to know each other better, to understand their school cultures better, and to listen more intently to their own inner voices. Other practices followed at the retreats included giving time for journaling and silence, raising questions and metaphors for engaged thinking, and allowing ample time to grapple with the nuances of paradox (Jackson and Jackson, 2002). I was honored to participate as one of two facilitators of the retreats, and I gathered data as the retreats progressed and ended.

External Partners

From 2006 through 2009, the partnership of the Fetzer Institute and Texas Wesleyan University served to provide funding for transformative professional development for teachers and school leaders. The Fetzer Institute has a remarkable history of funding individual and community health and wholeness projects. Its mission can be found at www.fetzer.org. Texas Wesleyan University (www.txwes.edu) offers recognized programs in teacher and school leader preparation and often collaborates in efforts that bring academic and healthy growth in learning communities.

The primary benefit of having these two organizations involved in professional development was one of funding for the specialized project. In addition, and as is true in many cases, the external partners expected research data that would support or clarify the project as valuable or not, for other teachers and school leaders. Therefore, research efforts focused on two areas that are important in public schools: the effect of transformative professional development on education outcomes, and the effect of transformative professional development on systems, particularly school culture. Other than helping to establish parameters for answering research questions, the two partners were not directly involved with the professional development project.

Overview of Transformative Professional Development Retreat Space

Each retreat was designed to follow the principles and practices of facilitation as highlighted in transformative professional learning theory (Mezirow, 1991) and demonstrated in Courage to Teach® programs and Circles of

NEW DIRECTIONS FOR TEACHING AND LEARNING • DOI: 10.1002/tl

Trust programs (Palmer, 2004, 2007), which include deep respect for the adult learner–participant and his or her inner voice and reflective reasoning. Both facilitators were trained in Courage to Teach® facilitation processes and had previous experience facilitating retreats in the Courage to Teach® programs. One premise of these programs is that "we trust each other to have the intention, discipline and good will to create and hold a space" that is safe, confidential, and that allows us "to speak our truth and to listen and respond to what we hear" (Palmer, 2004, p. 66). Growth in personal and professional understanding was invited, not mandated.

Each seasonal retreat's topic presented ways for participants to more fully reflect on their roles as teachers and school leaders, on how collaborations and connections are formed and deformed (Palmer, 2003), and to practice listening more deeply to others and to self. Themes for the five retreats were:

September: The Treasure, Seeds of the True Self
November: Bridges We Cross, Paths We Follow, Connecting to Community
February: Wintering Through: Dormancy, Solitude and Renewal
May: Embracing Paradox
September: Summer's Gifts, New Beginnings

Each retreat time began with the group gathering at the chosen setting at 5 p.m. on Friday afternoon. We enjoyed a relaxed meal together and participated in two discussion sessions. Then we met again on Saturday morning for continental breakfast, facilitated sessions, lunch, and more sessions. The retreat then ended by 5 p.m. Purposefully, the retreat space was kept informal yet in tune with the timed agenda and with an intentional slower pace. We allowed ourselves the gift of doing one thing at a time. The particular retreat venues gave participants a place of beauty and sereneness and a sense of separation from the usual busyness of their daily lives. Even menus, food, and text materials were chosen with care.

Examples of questions that we pondered individually in journals, in dyads and triads, or in large-group circles included:

"When did I first know I wanted to be a teacher, a principal, an educator?"

"Who is the person who teaches, who leads our school?"

"What new vision is abundantly growing in me? What is dying in me?"

"When has my relationship within my learning community allowed me to feel fully myself? When has it made me feel small?"

"Where do we see paradox in our lives? How do we respond to the tension of a paradox?"

"What new growth is evidenced in my school? Where are areas of change in direction or growth? What is dying in my school?"

For the retreat series, approximately sixty hours of professional development were available to each participant during the five retreats. Funding per person for participation in the five retreats averaged $1,600. Budgeted costs for all retreats included materials, venues, food, facilitation, mileage, travel, external evaluator, technology, and data collection support. By increasing numbers of participants and limiting costs of venues, external evaluation, technology, and data support, the per person cost could be decreased.

Overview of Research Results

To clarify the transformative professional development experience and to determine the value of such an experience, two research questions were answered:

1. What are the effects of a transformative professional development program on outcome variables important to public education, particularly upon a school's "report card" rating as reported in the Academic Excellence Indicator System and the Accountability Ratings System, issued each year by the State of Texas?
2. What are the effects of a transformative professional development program on system changes, particularly school organizational culture?

Each experimental group in each retreat series represented three schools, with a school leader and four teachers from his or her school. All participants were recruited and selected from schools rated no higher than "academically acceptable," as listed in the Texas Accountability Ratings System. Using Texas school report card measures (from State of Texas Academic Excellence Indicator System, Comparison Group Data, and Multi-History for 2003–2009) and a control group of three similar schools matched by the Texas Education Agency for comparison, the results of the project showed that test scores for each experimental school in the retreat cohorts increased slightly after the year of retreats, with state math scores increasing most. When compared with a control group of schools, the experimental group's state test scores also showed greater increase than the control group. However, the increases were not statistically significant.

In response to this finding, it would be difficult to pinpoint one strategy that alone increases a school's state test scores. Transformative professional development experiences such as a retreat series may be a strong link to increased test scores, yet they are one of many. Clearly, in Texas, many public school leaders and teachers are under extreme pressure for their students to perform at acceptable or higher levels on the criterion-referenced state tests (Booher-Jennings, 2004). Teachers of all grades volunteer or are required to give time for additional tutoring after school or on Saturdays; for writing, reading, and math camps; or for similar extra teaching duties. Much of the school day is spent in preparation for the tests as well. Because of the intense test preparation using multiple approaches, it would be difficult to identify one single element that increased state test scores during the three years of this project.

What can be said is that transformative professional development experiences provided teachers and school leaders purposeful time to develop cohesive talk about school issues, and certainly state testing is one issue of high anxiety. Our project, the Transformative Professional Development series of retreats, gave space and time for the school teams to develop relational trust, higher levels of optimism, and dialogue around such meaningful concerns.

Significant Results in Positive School Culture Ratings

Statistically significant increases were found in each cohort's pre- and postsurvey scores regarding their school cultures. Tables 7.1–7.4 present

Table 7.1. Significance in Total Year I, Year II, Year III School Culture Pre/Postprogram Surveys

Total Retreat Groups	Preprogram Survey, N = 45	Postprogram Survey, N = 34
Mean	81.18	88.06
$t(33) = -3.504, p < .001$		
Subscale: Teacher to Teacher Trust		
Mean	17.00	18.44
$t(33) = -2.522, p < .02$		
Subscale: Collective Responsibility		
Mean	19.68	22.59
$t(33) = -3.658, p < .001$		
Subscale: Commitment to School		
Mean	11.91	13.12
$t(33) = -2.425, p < .05$		

Table 7.2. Significance in Year I 2006–2007 Pre/Postprogram School Culture Surveys

	Preprogram Survey, N = 15	Postprogram Survey, N = 12
Subscale: Teacher to Teacher Trust		
Mean	17.67	19.83
$t(11) = -2.221, p < .05$		

Table 7.3. Significance in Year II 2007–2008 Pre/Postprogram School Culture Surveys

Total	Preprogram Survey, N = 15	Postprogram Survey, N = 11
Mean	71.27	84.00
$t(10) = -3.023, p < .02$		
Subscale: Teacher to Teacher Trust		
Mean	15.09	17.36
$t(10) = -2.231, p < .05$		
Subscale: Joint Problem Solving		
Mean	12.63	13.45
$t(10) = 1, ns$		
Subscale: Reflective Dialogue		
Mean	17.45	19.72
$t(10) = -2.231, p < .05$		
Subscale: Collective Responsibility		
Mean	16.45	21.73
$t(10) = -3.246, p < .01$		
Subscale: Commitment to School		
Mean	9.64	11.72
$t(10) = -2.681, p < .05$		

Table 7.4. Significance in Year III 2008–2009 Pre/Postprogram School Culture Surveys

Total	Preprogram Survey, N = 15	Postprogram Survey, N = 11
Mean	81.73	87.54
$t(10) = -2.284, p < .05$		
Subscale: Joint Problem Solving		
Mean	11.54	13.
$t(10) = -1.991, p < .08$		

evidence of statistically significant changes in all participants' school cultures, which were rated before the Transformative Professional Development retreats and then rated again after the retreats ended. Combining all of the participants (N = 45) for the three-year period, the data showed a statistically significant increase in the overall scores of school cultures, as well as in several of the subscales. Subscales that increased for all retreat participants' school cultures were "teacher to teacher trust," "collective responsibility," and "commitment to school." Tables 7.2–7.4 provide data on significant changes in each year's three school teams. The increases in school culture characteristics demonstrate positive results from the Transformative Professional Development series of retreats. Our School Culture survey, found in Appendix 7.1, is based on the work of the Chicago Annenberg Research Project (Smylie and others, 2003) and proved helpful in determining overall factors that contribute to a learning community's culture.

The school culture characteristics' positive growth may be attributed to the Transformative Professional Development series of retreats. For a school leader and his or her team of teachers to be given facilitated opportunities for self-reflection, for dialogue, and for building relationships away from the busy school environment speaks strongly for the possibilities of such programs to exist in schools and other educational settings. Time specifically given in each retreat for the school teams to have an uninterrupted dialogue upon the retreat topic and its application for their school was appreciated and rated highly valuable. The importance of improving school culture and relational trust cannot be overstated (Bryk and Schneider, 2002; Hargreaves and Fink, 2006). Everything that must happen for a learning community to grow, develop, and transform rests on how much its members learn to trust each other.

Other Learning About Transformative Professional Development

Additional, unexpected learning about transformative professional development is worth mentioning. Probably the single most difficult problem to solve in offering such programs is the tightrope dance that encourages participants to allot the necessary time commitment and yet keeps the program offering as invitational as possible. Allowing ample time for reflection, journaling, and listening to each other and one's inner voice requires that the process occur over time, such as a term or full year or even longer. However, for many educators this time commitment is difficult. The school leaders who were part of the retreats had the most difficulty being present for each retreat, as their school duties often required them to conduct Friday night or Saturday events. The spring semester state tests brought additional time conflicts for teachers due to required Saturday tutoring. Teachers and school leaders have family ties, interests beyond jobs, community and religious commitments, all of which involve time commitments. Yet, precisely when time is given to the process of transformative professional development with educators, the possibility of increased trust and positive school culture is greater.

We observed also that teachers and school leaders tend to have difficulty slowing down for the process of transformative professional development. In our retreats, the day's agenda and its activities such as reflective journaling or small group discussion moved slowly, purposefully. However, most activities in an educator's work day require him or her to make fast decisions and act promptly. The slower pace of the Transformative Professional Development was uncomfortable for some. Over time, we observed that participants developed an appreciation for the slower pace and a "wisdom" regarding when to make fast decisions, or not, during their daily lives.

Another unexpected dilemma and consequent learning occurred. The Transformative Professional Development series of retreats studied reported an unusually high turnover of school leaders during the retreat series or as the school year ended. Specifically, six of the nine school leaders left their school positions during or as the retreat series ended. It appeared from interviews that several school leaders moved from their positions as a result of having an opportunity to reflect on their daily work, which was not expected. Having time and space for dialogue and reflection created the possibility for these educators to reconsider their roles as educators and their positions, affirming or not, their school position.

Educator renewal from self-reflection is a benefit of transformative professional development retreats (Jurow, 2009). However, self-reflection may create the impetus for an educator to stay with or move from his or her position, and this possibility must be acknowledged. Interviews of school leaders revealed their reasoning concerning their work: "I came to realize I had a real purpose at this school," or "I came to realize that I could not stay in my school." Another leader said, "The district pressure for leading a school to success as expressed by higher test scores was not worth it, so I left."

Finally, the unusual mix of school leaders with teachers in the retreats began as a concern for many but came to be celebrated over time. Dialogue about their schools and sharing experiences with small groups and large groups in the retreats gave both teachers and school leaders insights into themselves and the "not so easy" roles of their colleagues. The participants noted that the invisible line of administrator versus teachers seemed to diminish, and the mix allowed them to develop more empathy and to learn from each other.

Summary

The Transformative Professional Development program as funded by external partners, the Fetzer Institute and Texas Wesleyan University, provided a possible model for future professional development. Although Texas state test scores in the nine schools of the project increased and experimental group scores increased more than control group scores for all tests, reading tests, and math tests, it would be difficult to assume that the Transformative Professional Development retreat series was the sole factor in improving test scores in any one school. Certainly, such a series of retreats, which honor the educator's professional and personal role in the educational process and which create safe space for reflection, is one factor among many. For educators to have the opportunity over a year to visit informally and respectfully with each other regarding the issues that face their schools is a valuable consideration.

More important is the positive effect of transformative professional development programs on school culture. In each of the experimental groups of the three Transformative Professional Development retreat series, positive change occurred significantly. Perhaps the improvement in school culture is also a possible reason for improvement in state test scores on each of the school campuses. Positive school culture provides impetus to innovative programs (Hargreaves and Fink, 2006), relational trust (Bryk and Schneider, 2002; Hoy and Tartar, 2004), and integrity in the classroom, hallways, and school offices. Negative school culture may give those who work and learn in school environments a dismal outlook, which in turn may lead to helplessness, hopelessness, and academic failure (Rothstein-Fisch and Trumbull, 2007). The reports of greater trust, responsibility, and commitment to school were signs of transformation in school cultures, which in turn may make greater differences in students' lives.

References

Booher-Jennings, J. "Responding to the Texas Accountability System: The Erosion of Relational Trust." Paper presented at the annual meeting of the American Sociological

Association, San Francisco, CA, 2004. Retrieved May 26, 2009 from http://allacademic.com/meta/p109907_index.html.

Bryk, A. S., and Schneider, B. *Trust in Schools: A Core Resource for Improvement*. New York: Sage Publications, 2002.

Cranton, P. *Understanding and Promoting Transformative Learning: A Guide for Educators of Adults*. San Francisco: Jossey-Bass, 1994.

Hargreaves, A., and Fink, D. *Sustainable Leadership*. San Francisco: Wiley, 2006.

Hoy, W., and Tartar, J. C. "Organizational Justice in Schools: No Justice Without Trust." *International Journal of Educational Management*, 2004, *18*, 250–259.

Jackson, M., and Jackson, R. "Courage to Teach®: A Retreat Program of Personal and Professional Renewal for Educators." In S. Intrator (ed.), *Stories of the Courage to Teach®: Honoring the Teacher's Heart* (pp. 282–308). San Francisco: Jossey-Bass, 2002.

Jurow, A. S. "Cultivating Self in the Context of Transformative Professional Development." *Journal of Teacher Education*, 2009, *60*(3), 277–290.

Kitchenham, A. "The Evolution of John Mezirow's Transformative Learning Theory." *Journal of Transformative Education*, 2008, *6*(2), 104–123. doi: 10.1177/1541 344608322678.

Mezirow, J. *Transformative Dimensions of Adult Learning*. San Francisco: Jossey-Bass, 1991.

Palmer, P. J. "Teaching with Heart and Soul: Reflections on Spirituality in Teacher Education." *Journal of Teacher Education*, 2003, *54*, 376–385.

Palmer, P. J. *A Hidden Wholeness: The Journey Toward an Undivided Life*. San Francisco: Jossey-Bass, 2004.

Palmer, P. J. *The Courage to Teach: Exploring the Inner Landscape of a Teacher's Life*. San Francisco: Jossey-Bass, 2007.

Rothstein-Fisch, C., and Trumbull, E. *Managing Diverse Classrooms: How to Build on Students' Cultural Strengths*. Baltimore: Association for Supervision and Curriculum Development, 2007.

Scott, S M. "The Grieving Soul in the Transformation Process." In P. Cranton (ed.), *Transformative Learning in Action: Insights from Practice*. New Directions for Adult and Continuing Education, no. 74. San Francisco: Jossey-Bass, 1997.doi: 10.1002 /ace.7405.

Smylie, M., and others. *The Chicago Annenberg Challenge: Successes, Failures and Lessons for the Future*. Final technical report of the Chicago Annenberg Research Project. Chicago: Consortium on Chicago School Research, 2003.

TWYLA T. MIRANDA serves as editor of the Wesleyan Graduate Review *and teaches in the graduate programs at Texas Wesleyan University. She may be reached at tmiranda@txwes.edu.*

NEW DIRECTIONS FOR TEACHING AND LEARNING • DOI: 10.1002/tl

Appendix 7.1. School Culture—Educator Questionnaire

Rate each item with 1–4 in the line beside the item.

1 means strongly disagree.
2 means disagree.
3 means agree.
4 means strongly agree.

Teacher to Teacher Relational Trust

_____ Most teachers really care about each other.
_____ Teachers trust each other.
_____ It's OK to discuss feelings and worries with other teachers.
_____ Teachers respect colleagues who lead school improvement efforts.
_____ Teachers respect those colleagues who are expert at their craft.
_____ We feel respect from other teachers.

Joint Problem Solving

_____ Faculty meetings are often used for problem solving.
_____ The faculty has a good process for making group decisions.
_____ Many teachers express their personal views at faculty meetings.
_____ We do a good job talking through views/opinions/values.
_____ When a conflict arises, we [don't] "sweep it under the rug."

Reflective Dialogue

_____ Conversations about the school's goals occur more than twice a month.
_____ Conversations about curriculum development occur more than twice a month.
_____ Conversations about managing class behavior occur more than twice a month.
_____ Conversations about what helps students learn best occur more than twice a month.
_____ Teachers regularly discuss assumptions about teaching and learning.
_____ Teachers share and discuss student work with other teachers.
_____ Teachers talk about instruction in the teachers' lounge.

Collective Responsibility

_____ Feel responsible when students fail.
_____ Feel responsible to help each other do their best.
_____ Help maintain discipline in the entire school.
_____ Take responsibility for improving the school.
_____ Feel responsible for helping students develop self-control.

_____ Set high standards for ourselves.
_____ Feel responsible that all students learn.

Commitment to School

_____ Wouldn't want to work in any other school.
_____ Would recommend this school to parents.
_____ Often look forward to each working day at this school.
_____ Feel loyal to this school.

Additional information

1. What is your gender? Male_____ Female_____
2. What is your age? _____ years old
3. Number of years teaching _____ years
4. Number of years in school leadership _____years
5. What is primary responsibility in your school?

_____

6. Rate your level of optimism about your future career in education.

Very optimistic				Optimistic				Not Optimistic		
10	9	8	7	6	5	4	3	2	1	0

(survey based on assessments from the Chicago Annenberg Research Project, Smylie and others, 2003)

8

This chapter explores how utilizing the principles and practices of the Circle of Trust® approach helped to lay a generative foundation for democratic education in service of community healing and transformation in Mississippi.

Circles of Learning in Mississippi: Community Recovery and Democracy Building

Bonnie Allen, Estrus Tucker

Education must be born of the creative tension between how life is lived and how life might be lived in a free society.

—Adams, 1975, p. xv

In the aftermath of Hurricane Katrina, a synchronistic set of events and relationships generated a new kind of experiential learning in communities across Mississippi. Educators based at the University of Mississippi, community-based educators, social justice advocates, and funders collaborated to provide the resources and opportunities for diverse groups of Mississippians to participate in the Circle of Trust® approach as a vehicle for community healing and transformation. Created by educator and public intellectual Parker J. Palmer and the Center for Courage & Renewal (www.couragerenewal.org), this approach is a retreat-based learning format founded on a set of principles and practices that honor the cultivation of one's own wisdom and voice and evoke the courage to integrate the inner life with the active life of service and leadership. The theory of change behind the Circle of Trust® approach is that individual hearts and minds must open to new possibilities if external systems and structures are going to shift.

This chapter describes how these circles offer fresh approaches to "outside the classroom" teaching and learning about community recovery

NEW DIRECTIONS FOR TEACHING AND LEARNING, no. 130, Summer 2012 © Wiley Periodicals, Inc.
Published online in Wiley Online Library (wileyonlinelibrary.com) • DOI: 10.1002/tl.20020

and its relationship to democracy building. We discuss recovery both in the acute disaster recovery context and in the underlying, historic context of chronic recovery from deeply entrenched racism and poverty that many American communities face. By linking the fields of community recovery and education, we contend that community is central to pedagogy, as posited by Parker Palmer (1993, pp. xvii–xviii) in *To Know as We Are Known*:

> The central question of ethics in education is whether we are educating students in ways that make them responsive to the claims of community upon their lives. Are they simply learning to compete for scarce resources as isolated individuals, or are they learning how to create communities of abundance ... both as learners and as citizens?

The authors, as facilitators of the Circle of Trust® approach, share a perspective on how these educational experiences are creating new foundations for local democracy building in Mississippi, our nation's poorest state, with its notoriously undemocratic history. From the beginning, we approached our work in these circles with questions instead of answers, and an openness to the possibilities and resources of the human heart engaged. Well aware of the countless models of social change that have been attempted and failed in Mississippi, we humbly embraced a line of inquiry that asked whether these circles, embedded in grassroots communities and part of broader social change movements, could create atmospheres capable of fostering the imagination and courage needed to initiate lasting transformation. Could the principles and practices learned and experienced in these circles help cultivate new habits and skills among local leaders—attributes that would translate into empowered communities capable of determining their own futures by active engagement in democratic decision making?

Our hope is that the inquiry and experience in Mississippi will pique the curiosity of institutional educators and community leaders elsewhere. We encourage others to explore the Circle of Trust® approach as a way of breaking down the walls between theory and practice and bringing the rich resources of academic institutions to the community table where people live and work. In the words of Myles Horton, founder of the Highlander Folk School in the Tennessee mountains:

> If we are to think seriously about liberating people to cope with their own lives ... the bars must come down; the doors must fly open; nonacademic life—real life—must be encompassed by education. Multiple approaches must be invented; each one considered education in its own right. Education, in truth, can never be reduced to or confined within a system. (Jacobs, 2003, p. 242)

The Community Recovery Frame

"Community recovery" is an emerging interdisciplinary field drawing on theory and practice from a broad range of disciplines, including sociology, psychology, economics, political science, law, planning, engineering, ecology, and health. An aspect of community development, it includes the study of conditions that either catalyze or block the healthy development of the social, as well as physical, infrastructure needed for communities to thrive, prosper, and determine their own futures in the wake of a crisis.

As referenced in this article, "community recovery" is much more than simply returning to the status quo before a disaster. It includes but goes beyond resilience: the ability of a person or a place to bounce back from a traumatic blow. We also discuss recovery from chronic disaster: the "disaster before the disaster" in the case of Hurricane Katrina striking a region already devastated by poverty and racial inequity. A study by the Community and Regional Resilience Institute amassed forty-five different definitions of resilience in contemporary research, suggesting great fluidity in the art and science of this capacity (Plodinec, 2009).

We contend that within this fluidity is an expanded understanding of community recovery: one that uncovers the hidden assets, dreams, and possibilities of residents for individual and collective transformation. The status of many communities in Mississippi before the storm was far from idyllic. Just as in many other parts of our nation, low-wealth Mississippians and communities of color are seeking to recover from economic disinvestment, staggering job losses, public health threats, violence, and deep poverty. Structural racism is alive and well, continuing to shape systems, structures, and public policies in Mississippi and across America.

For our purposes, then, "community recovery and democracy building" is a frame for transformative learning and action to create new community narratives. In this context, the Circle of Trust® approach does not provide a blueprint for social change. Instead, it provides a quality of process that bends toward democracy, thus allowing the participants to write the story themselves with a radical openness to possibility.

The authors write from the standpoint of native Southerners with long histories of social justice advocacy. Somewhere along the way, we came to understand that activism alone would not create the social change we sought. With backgrounds in law and community organizing, we discovered the writings of Parker Palmer in the 1990s, fortuitously providing new insights into a social justice field increasingly wrought by discouragement. Despite the good intentions and hard work of many social justice activists, the countless academic studies of community change, and the millions upon millions of philanthropic dollars invested, many nonprofit leaders, educators, and funders are deeply frustrated by the failure of their efforts to "move the dial" on daunting social problems. For this reason, a growing number of funders and institutions, including the Fetzer Institute, Kellogg Foundation, Seasons Fund, Foundation for the Mid South, Center for Courage & Renewal, Mississippi Center for Justice, Steps Coalition, and Winter Institute for Racial Reconciliation, are offering new approaches to social change that address the roots of human suffering lodged deep in the human heart—where the seeds for transformation also rest. Each of these organizations invested in Mississippi as a place to test these approaches.

The authors are seasoned community educators in the popular education tradition where "theory fertilizes purposeful action and action puts theory to the test" (Jacobs, 2003, p. 247). Popular education is no stranger to Mississippi, with its history of Freedom Schools and ground zero for the Civil Rights Movement. Building on this rich history, we narrate the story in real time, as it organically continues to unfold, of why we and our partners chose this particular model of popular education at this time and in this place; the values, principles, and practices upon which it stands; who has participated in the circles; and the transformative experiences we have witnessed. We also reflect on the application of the Circle of Trust® approach on a broader scale to teaching and learning about conditions for building democracy.

Why Mississippi?

The crisis of Katrina provided an optimal moment for democratic education. The shocking failure of the federal government to respond adequately to this mammoth disaster gave rise to a new urgency for local problem solving. Although the recovery process (and the distribution of federal recovery dollars) proved to be highly inequitable over the long run, the immediate impact of the storm had a leveling effect. Rich and poor and black, brown, and white together lost the lives of loved ones, were rendered homeless, and lived in tents and Federal Emergency Management Agency trailers for months and years. This environment provided a unique opportunity for the Circle of Trust® approach to serve as a safe space container that allowed diverse sets of survivors to share their stories and explore their own resourcefulness.

Hurricane Katrina struck the Mississippi Gulf Coast in August 2005 as this country's most destructive natural disaster. Hundreds of thousands of homes were crushed in Katrina's wake, along with neighborhoods and generations of a way of life, decimating every stretch of Mississippi's eighty-mile coastline. During the next several days, the eyes of the nation watched in horror as a deadly second round of disaster unfolded in New Orleans: a perfect storm of broken levees and thousands of poor, elderly, disabled, and mostly African-American residents blatantly left behind. The world bore witness in shock and disbelief to the rapid

NEW DIRECTIONS FOR TEACHING AND LEARNING • DOI: 10.1002/tl

unraveling of a civil society, shattering the myth of America as an invincible democracy.

More than one in five Mississippians lives at or below the federal poverty level. Mississippi also has the highest percentage of African-Americans (37 percent). Despite tremendous progress made as a result of the Civil Rights Movement, many vestiges of the institutions and systems that existed during Mississippi's plantation era have survived into the twenty-first century and result in dismal prospects for high numbers of Mississippians today. Year after year, Mississippi continues to rank last in health and most other human development indicators (Burd-Sharps, Lewis, and Martins, 2009).

The authors first came to Mississippi in the wake of Katrina, along with thousands of other volunteers, scholars, students, and practitioners of every discipline. Bonnie Allen traveled from the Fetzer Institute in Michigan to Mississippi to serve as a legal volunteer for the Mississippi Center for Justice. Estrus Tucker traveled from his home state of Texas to facilitate various forms of community recovery retreats. What we found is a paradoxical culture that makes Mississippi an ideal learning laboratory for community recovery and democracy building.

Mississippi is a part of the world both cursed and charmed by a history of unthinkable suffering, violence, and hatred, alongside extraordinary hospitality, generosity, and courage. Outsiders are awestruck by the open-arm welcome they receive from Mississippians of all races and classes. They also experience firsthand the vast richness of Mississippi's culture in music, literature, spirituality, and cuisine. In stark contrast, however, the state is notorious for patterns of governmental decisions that offer little hospitality to the state's most vulnerable residents. Mississippi's toxic policy environment seems designed to keep poor people in poverty, rather than provide them with the tools to build wealth and opportunity. Why private acts of generosity do not translate into public policy is a burning question in Mississippi and other parts of the Deep South.

The silver lining of Katrina is that enormous sums of funding, volunteers, and other resources poured in from foundations, corporations, national nonprofits, and churches. Colleges, universities, and professional schools sent teams of faculty, researchers, and students to study community recovery from various disciplines and to provide technical assistance. This infusion of resources and partners created new possibilities for coastal Mississippi. New organizations were born and new leaders emerged. Katrina put a region of the state obscured from the prevailing civil rights narrative "on the map." Many Americans did not even realize Mississippi had a coastline before the national spotlight focused on the sleepy towns of Long Beach, Bay St. Louis, Pass Christian, Biloxi, and many others that dot Mississippi's Gulf Coast. All of these factors combined to create a ripe new venue for theorists and practitioners to study and participate in community recovery.

NEW DIRECTIONS FOR TEACHING AND LEARNING • DOI: 10.1002/tl

A Collaborative Approach to Education—Inside and Outside the Academy

As Katrina survivors on the Mississippi Gulf Coast began to climb out of the rubble, new approaches to racial reconciliation were emerging in other parts of the state. In 2005, the William Winter Institute for Racial Reconciliation, based at the University of Mississippi, began to convene citizens from diverse faith, professional, and social communities to explore what Mississippi might look like if it were a social justice state, a place where fairness, respect, and equal treatment under the law reigned.

The Winter Institute was founded in 1999, following President Clinton's One America Initiative on Race. Former Mississippi Governor William Winter played a lead role in One America, and the University of Mississippi hosted the only Deep South public forum for the president's initiative. Governor Winter is well known for his role in leading the charge for publicly funded primary education in Mississippi.

The institute is grounded in the University of Mississippi's history, and believes that the university has a unique responsibility and opportunity to foster racial reconciliation and the scholarly study of race and racism. The institute contends that if the university is to achieve its goal as a great American public university for the twenty-first century, it must expand its definition of education beyond classroom teaching and campus research. It must include community service and embrace the opportunity to educate and serve the community and citizenry beyond the university. The institute also believes that education is a collaborative process and that all involved are both educators and educated, especially when scholarly research, study, and teaching are complemented by service.

Out of this mission the Winter Institute spearheaded the Mississippi Welcome Table Project to promote community dialogue with the hope of planting seeds of justice across the state. Participants believed that change comes through dialogue and relationship building, followed by effective community action. In June 2006, the group kicked off a year of dialogue around the state with a gathering of over 300 citizens at the state capitol. Dialogue projects began in each of the four congressional districts over the next year. Enough of those present recognized a great need to build the capacity of citizens to engage in dialogues addressing race and racism effectively.

With support from the Fetzer Institute and the W. K. Kellogg Foundation, the Winter Institute initiated an era of dialogue on race, beginning with a pilot training program in the fall of 2008, and continuing with a twelve- to eighteen-month statewide training program started in the fall of 2009. A great diversity of facilitators, storytellers, and community practitioners collaborated with staff and interns of the Winter Institute and resident leaders to design, refine, and guide the emerging process. Several Circle of Trust® approach facilitators participated, including the authors.

We began with the Generosity of Spirit model that features cross-cultural storytelling to reveal and promote generosity, an appreciation of participant personal stories, and the liberation of gifts. Mark Nepo, a former program officer at the Fetzer Institute, led a national team that developed curriculum for retreat gatherings based on over 200 teaching stories culled from many different cultures and folk traditions. Specific group norms kindred to Circle of Trust® approach practices were modeled by lead facilitators and gradually became the container for the developing process of dialogue, planning, and action. Over time the Generosity of Spirit retreats were integrated into the Welcome Table Project and morphed into a version of the Circle of Trust® approach, tailored to the context of why these particular participants were convening and what they hoped to learn.

Beginning in January 2010, the Welcome Table moved into five Mississippi communities. Local community leaders and residents from each community participated in a two-and-a-half-day retreat, followed by dialogue, planning, and action in each community over the course of the year, led by the residents with support from the facilitation team, staff, and interns of the Winter Institute. The facilitation team is currently designing a harvesting retreat for representatives from the five local communities. The planning team will discern lessons from this phase and suggest next steps for a ten-year initiative.

The Welcome Table Project was an interesting parallel to the application of the Circle of Trust® approach to Katrina recovery. Although the former arose in a higher education context (the University of Mississippi's leveraging its resources by partnering with community leaders on racial reconciliation), the Circle of Trust® approach emerged on the Mississippi Gulf Coast from grassroots leaders who recognized the need for recovery of the human spirit as well as bricks and mortar and building new relationships across class and race. Fortuitously, the Foundation for the Mid South announced a Resiliency Grants initiative in partnership with the American Red Cross in 2007. The Mississippi Center for Justice received a grant to sponsor a series of retreats for diverse groups of caregivers, social advocates, and residents. Subsequently, the Steps Coalition, a coalition of over thirty-five nonprofits formed in the aftermath of Katrina to advance a healthy, equitable, and just recovery, secured funding from the Seasons Fund for additional retreats that focused on the Courage to Lead®—again, based on the Circle of Trust® Approach.

This convergence of funding opportunities and the will of leaders on the ground provided the opportunity for parallel tracks to proceed. All of the sponsoring organizations—the Mississippi Center for Justice, Steps Coalition, and Winter Institute—adhere to particular core values and beliefs that are compatible and complimentary to the core values, principles, and practices underlying the Circle of Trust® approach. The Mississippi Center for Justice uses a deeply relational "community lawyering" model of advocacy to advance racial and economic justice through systemic change. Steps' members work to transform systems, structures, and policies affecting five social justice pillars: affordable housing, environmental justice, jobs and economic justice, preservation of historic communities, and human rights. Across these issues, Steps sees its mission as developing local leadership, empowering communities to advocate for themselves, and facilitating collaboration. Steps and the Mississippi Center for Justice are in the early stages of creating a Mississippi Gulf Coast Democracy School with a youth component leading the way. The principles and practices of the Circle of Trust® approach will be foundational in forming the vision and programming for the Democracy School.

Core values and principles of the Winter Institute include:

- America has been, is now, and increasingly will be a multiracial nation. But racism has diminished every aspect of our society. We have no choice but to speak the truth about race and racism, and seek equality, justice, and reconciliation.
- Despite the tragedies of the past, or perhaps because of them, both black and white Mississippians and Southerners have a profound sense of place, of being rooted in our neighborhoods and local communities. It is fitting to focus special attention on local community and grassroots reconciliation between blacks and whites.
- Racial reconciliation requires individual, person-to-person respect for those who are "other" than us, and mutual respect, fairness, and equity in all dealings with those who are different or "other."
- Individual and group respect, equal access and opportunity, and justice are inextricably connected to and essential for community wellness and broad-based multiracial economic growth.
- Reconciliation is a participatory process that requires choices and democratic decision making from the ground up, one person, one community, and one organization at a time.
- Individuals and communities have to heal themselves. Reconciliation cannot be imposed from the outside or top down.

Creating Conditions for Democratic Education

Given the historical context of Mississippi and the missions of the Mississippi Center for Justice, Steps Coalition, and the Winter Institute, a particular kind of learning space and process was needed to lay the foundation for democratic education in service of community healing and transformation. In Parker Palmer's words:

> The quality of the process you use to get to a place determines the ends, so when you want to build a democratic society, you have to act democratically in every way. If you want love and brotherhood, you've got to incorporate them as you go along, because you can't just expect them to occur in the future without experiencing them before you get there. (Horton, 1997, p. 227)

NEW DIRECTIONS FOR TEACHING AND LEARNING • DOI: 10.1002/tl

Palmer (1993, p. 71) mirrors this concept of the "quality of process" when he describes a "learning space" with three essential characteristics: openness, boundaries and hospitality. Creating *open* space means removing impediments to learning that we find around and within us, including the fear of not knowing. It also means arranging the learning place where teachers and learners sit in a circle as equal participants. Creating *bounded* space means using learning texts and other "third things" that serve as a container for reflection, a fixed time and space for seeing and hearing one's own truth and the truth of others. Creating *hospitable* space means receiving each other, our struggles, our newborn ideas, with openness and care. These classrooms are "places where every stranger and strange utterance is met with welcome" (Palmer, 1993, p. 74).

Palmer developed the Circle of Trust® approach to honor these essential characteristics of learning spaces. In *A Hidden Wholeness*, he writes about embracing the challenge of becoming whole:

> But we cannot embrace that challenge all alone, at least, not for long: we need trustworthy relationships, tenacious communities of support, if we are to sustain the journey toward an undivided life. (Palmer, 2004, p. 10)

The Circle of Trust® approach creates a shared space safe for engagement that enables participants to reconnect who they are with what they do and approach their lives and work with renewed passion, commitment, and integrity. So it is in the context of community recovery, where we invited and engaged people who dared to believe in the innate and irrepressible value of engaging their neighbors and their stories despite the dominant narratives of politics, power, and textbook history, that we introduced the Circle of Trust® approach in Mississippi. Our retreats' creative use of poetry, stories, solitude, reflection, open and honest questions, and deep listening was well received by professional and nonprofessional, highly and minimally educated participants. In addition to advancing the work in Mississippi, we believed that this community recovery context for the Circle of Trust® approach would contribute significantly to the growing national conversation about reclaiming integrity and courage in professional and public life, particularly with diverse educational, economic, and nonprofessional backgrounds.

As we carefully designed our retreats in Mississippi, being mindful of the cross-section of resident and leader voices, the values underlying the Circle of Trust® approach were deeply informative and resonated in the stories and engagement of participants, including:

Diversity. The capacity to welcome and make space for diverse voices and multiple perspectives is critical to the healing and wholeness needed in our world.

NEW DIRECTIONS FOR TEACHING AND LEARNING • DOI: 10.1002/tl

Community. "Inner work" is not simply a focus on ourselves. Rather, it enables individuals to become more aware of the fabric of connectedness with others, generating an ongoing sense of responsibility and stewardship.

Love. It is the grounding of our work, by which we mean the capacity to extend ourselves for the sake of another person's growth. Our work in community stretches us to understand, respect, and support each other, teaching us why learning to love is one of the most demanding disciplines we can choose.

Hope. We believe and act on our most dearly held dreams, persisting even when the odds are against them. In the midst of the despair and brokenheartedness experienced by so many in our world today, our work engenders hope for people to live purposeful lives, do meaningful work, and make contributions to succeeding generations.

These values were formative as Parker Palmer and the Center for Courage & Renewal developed specific principles and practices to create certain conditions in the Circle of Trust® approach. Those foremost in our Mississippi retreat settings include:

- Creating open and hospitable space that invites us to slow down, listen, and reflect. At the same time, we engage in dialogue with others in the circle about things that matter. As this "sorting and sifting" goes on, we are able to clarify and affirm our truth in the presence of others, and that truth is more likely to overflow into our work and community leadership.
- Committing to no fixing, advising, "saving," or setting each other straight. This simple rule honors the primacy and integrity of the inner teacher. When we are free from external judgment, we are more likely to have an honest conversation with ourselves and learn to check and correct ourselves from within.
- Asking honest open questions to "hear each other into speech." Instead of advising each other, we learn to listen deeply and ask questions that help others hear their own inner wisdom more clearly.
- Exploring the intersection of the universal stories of human experience with the personal stories of our lives through poetry, teaching stories, music, or works of art drawn from diverse cultures and wisdom traditions. This invites us to reflect on the "big questions" of our individual and shared lives.
- Using multiple modes of reflection so everyone can find his or her place and pace. We explore important questions in large group conversation and dialogues in small groups. We make time for individual reflection and journaling, and we honor the educative power of silence.
- Honoring confidentiality by understanding that nothing said in these circles will be revealed outside the circle and that things said by

participants will not be pursued when a session ends, unless the speaker requests it.

What We Are Learning About Transformation

Ultimately, the goal of education is transformation: unleashing potential and changing the range of possibilities for teachers and learners through expanded knowledge and imagination. As transformed learners move out into the world, they become agents for changing their institutions and communities. At the heart of education—as discussed in this chapter—is democracy: both as a means and an end. Democratic practices in the course of education promote democratic practices in community.

The democratic conditions we are trying to create in Mississippi have produced many transformative moments. We have heard personal stories reflecting a broad range of applications and the far-reaching influences of our hospitable and disciplined learning space. One participant, a seasoned activist, vowed to practice our touchstones (group norms) at every meeting and also in her home because they completely change her way of leading, serving, and interacting with others. A young adult student expressed how impressed he was with the conviction and resiliency of a grandmother in the circle, and although she was of a different race and background, she embodied the same values and grace of his own beloved grandmother. A former mayor admitted that if his fellow elected leaders and staff had half the level of trust experienced in this circle he would still be in office.

Of course, transformation is not measured in a snapshot or an isolated moment but throughout the succession of new and more wholehearted ways of being and doing, creative approaches to persistent problems, and the demonstrable use of diverse human capital in community. The slow work of community recovery and transformation, like democracy, is messy business. It takes patience, courage, hope, and a willingness to till the soil and plant seeds for a long time. As much emphasis as our educational systems place on intellectual development, education is at its core an enterprise of the heart. Parker Palmer writes in *The Courage to Teach: Exploring the Inner Landscape of a Teacher's Life* that "reform will never be achieved … if we fail to cherish—and challenge—the human heart that is the source of good teaching (1998, p. 4).

This wisdom also applies to the noble struggle for the common good, sustaining positive social change and creating a society that works for all. No amount of grant funding, tax breaks, business approaches, charitable investment, nonprofit advocacy, new programming, community building, service learning projects, or research will do any lasting good if we fail to honor, respect, and listen to our collective humanity, excluding no one. Indeed, daring to cherish and challenge the common ground of our human hearts may very well be the source of our human and community recovery, and the best hope for the fulfillment of democracy's promise.

NEW DIRECTIONS FOR TEACHING AND LEARNING • DOI: 10.1002/tl

We close with the wise words of Terry Tempest Williams:

> The human heart is the first home of democracy. It is where we embrace our questions: Can we be equitable? Can we be generous? Can we listen with our whole beings, not just our minds, and offer our attention rather than our opinion? And do we have enough resolve in our hearts to act courageously, relentlessly, without giving up—ever—trusting our fellow citizens to join us in our determined pursuit of a living democracy? (Williams, 2004, pp. 83–84)

References

Adams, F. *Unearthing Seeds of Fire: The Idea of Highlander.* Winston Salem, N.C.: John F. Blair, 1975.

Burd-Sharps, S., Lewis, K., and Martins, E. B. *A Portrait of Mississippi.* New York: American Human Development Project, 2009.

Horton, M. *The Long Haul: An Autobiography.* New York: Teachers College Press, Columbia University, 1997.

Jacobs, D. (ed.). *The Myles Horton Reader: Education for Social Change.* Knoxville, Tenn.: University of Tennessee Press, 2003.

Palmer, P. J. *To Know as We Are Known: Education as a Spiritual Journey.* New York: HarperCollins, 1993.

Palmer, P. J. *The Courage to Teach: Exploring the Inner Landscape of a Teacher's Life.* San Francisco: Jossey-Bass, 1998.

Palmer, P. J. *A Hidden Wholeness: The Journey Toward an Undivided Life.* San Francisco: Jossey-Bass, 2004.

Plodinec, M. J. *Definitions of Resilience: An Analysis.* Oak Ridge, Tenn.: Community and Regional Resilience Institute, 2009.

Williams, T. T. *The Open Space of Democracy.* Barrington, Mass.: The Orion Society, 2004.

BONNIE ALLEN is director of Access to Justice Partnerships at the Mississippi Center for Justice. She also has an independent consulting practice focused on community leadership and resource development. She holds a law degree from the University of Florida College of Law and a Master's Degree in theological studies from Garrett-Evangelical Theological Seminary.

ESTRUS TUCKER is an independent consultant and keynote speaker specializing in facilitation, designing and leading conversations and retreats around the country in service of personal, professional and community renewal, transformation, healing, reconciliation, and creative civic engagement. He is an alumnus of the University of Texas at Arlington, and the John Ben Shepherd Texas Public Leadership Forum.

NEW DIRECTIONS FOR TEACHING AND LEARNING • DOI: 10.1002/tl

This chapter reports the findings of an evaluation that explored the impact of Circle of Trust retreats and the learning and personal and professional applications in the lives of retreat participants. The Center for Courage & Renewal began offering Circle of Trust cross-professional retreats in 2005 to provide people from any profession with an opportunity to experience a "circle of trust" as described by Parker J. Palmer in his 2004 book, A Hidden Wholeness: The Journey Toward an Undivided Life.

Measuring the Impact of the Circle of Trust® Approach

Janet Smith

History of Circle of Trust Retreats

In the early 1990s, Parker J. Palmer created and developed the Courage to Teach® (CTT) series of retreats in Kalamazoo, Michigan, with the assistance and support of the Fetzer Institute. This series of retreats was designed for teachers grounded in an approach to professional development known as teacher "formation." The formation process focuses on the inner lives, personal renewal, and reflective practice of teachers rather than on teaching skills or knowledge. In 1996–1998, CTT retreats were successfully piloted in four locations across the United States. In 1997, the Fetzer Institute established the Center for Teacher Formation (CTF) to expand this work and prepare facilitators. The work gained further momentum with the publication of Palmer's book *The Courage to Teach: Exploring the Inner Landscape of a Teacher's Life* in 1998. CTT retreats grew in number and popularity over the ensuing years, and large numbers of CTT facilitators were trained. A 2002 external longitudinal evaluation of CTT noted that "the evaluation data establishes the CTT program as an exemplary and unique model of professional development" (Intrator and Scribner, 2002, p. 12).

As the success of the work with K–12 educators became more widely known, people in other serving professions also began to ask to be included in these formation retreats. In 2003, in response to the growing interest in

NEW DIRECTIONS FOR TEACHING AND LEARNING, no. 130, Summer 2012 © Wiley Periodicals, Inc.
Published online in Wiley Online Library (wileyonlinelibrary.com) • DOI: 10.1002/tl.20021

formation work from other serving professions, a cross-professional Courage & Renewal Facilitator Preparation Program was piloted. The 2004 publication of Palmer's book *A Hidden Wholeness: The Journey Toward an Undivided Life* further publicized this work and created an increased demand for retreats in other professions. Consequently, five national cross-professional retreats were offered during 2005. Due to the expansion of this work to other professions, in 2005 the CTF became the Center for Courage & Renewal (CCR; http://www.couragerenewal.org). Since then, the center has maintained an abiding commitment to education but also offers retreats to people in other professions, through some programs focusing on a specific profession, and others that work across professions. In 2006, a three-tiered cross-professional series of Circle of Trust (COT; http://www.couragerenewal.org/about/foundations) retreats was developed:

Introductory retreat: The Journey toward an Undivided Life (three days)

Intermediate retreat: Living the Questions, for people who have already attended an Introductory Circle of Trust retreat (four days)

Advanced retreat: Welcoming the Soul and Weaving Community, for people who have already attended an Introductory and Intermediate Circle of Trust retreat (four days)

Since the first Circle of Trust retreat was offered in 2005, the CCR and other individual facilitators across the United States, Canada, and Australia have continued to offer many cross-professional retreats, as they have proven extremely popular. They are designed for people from any profession who want to deepen their interactions and conversations in their workplaces, relationships, and communities. They also enable people who have read Palmer's *A Hidden Wholeness,* which outlines the principles of a circle of trust, to experience a circle and to understand more about the conditions that help create such circles. Palmer says that the purpose of a circle of trust "is to support the inner journey of each person in the group, to make each soul feel safe enough to show up and speak its truth, to help each person listen to his or her inner teacher" (Palmer, 2004, p. 54).

Although each of the Circle of Trust retreats has a slightly different focus, there are strong commonalities between all three retreats and also with all retreats offered by CCR. Courage & Renewal retreats, including Courage to Teach® and Courage to Lead®, involve creating Circles of Trust® and aim to provide people with the opportunity to "rejoin soul and role" or "reconnect who they are with what they do." Circle of Trust retreat facilitators seek to create spaces that are safe, quiet, focused, and inviting, so that participants can begin to hear their own inner voice. In large group, small group, and solitary settings, participants explore the intersection of their personal and professional lives, using stories from their own journeys, reflecting on their work and practice, and using insights from poets, storytellers, and various wisdom traditions. Other characteristics of Circle of Trust retreats include the use of silence, reflection, asking honest and open questions, clearness committees and "third" things such as poetry, prose, and metaphor. Each of the Circle of Trust retreats includes guidelines, sometimes called touchstones or boundary markers, that establish norms and respectful boundaries for working together.

Reflective Practice as a Form of Professional Development

There are currently many different types of professional development (PD) offerings within the serving professions, ranging from didactic and skills based to values and meanings based. Reflective practice is a form of PD found within the latter category, and Circle of Trust retreats are also located within this genre of PD, as they allow people to engage in professional renewal, reflection, and attentive presence about their professional and personal practice and sense of vocation. Reflective practice PD is now firmly established as a legitimate form of PD across all serving professions, and has also become very common and popular within the field of personal development. The various subsections of the reflective practice genre of PD are known as transformative work, professional renewal, lifelong learning, inner work, self-awareness, self-development, critique of practice, and critical thinking. The field of adult education is now firmly based on principles such as active and reflective inquiry rather than prior notions of passive reception of transmitted content (Knowles, 1990). It should be noted that reflective practice within the serving professions is also learned in ways other than professional development. For example, reflection is a fundamental tenet of practices such as mentoring, action research, and critical friendships.

Reflective practice is essentially a way of helping practitioners participate in a critique of their professional and personal practice in order to achieve better understandings about what they know and do and to learn through questioning (Day, 1999). It also involves careful consideration of both seeing and action to enhance the possibilities of learning through experience and the ability to frame and reframe the practice setting so that the practitioners' wisdom-in-action is enhanced (Loughran, 2002). The key characteristics of reflective practice professional development are the use of small group and large group conversations and dialogue; silence; storytelling; documentation of journey; reflective journaling and guided reflection; use of artifacts, poetry, art, and music; and attention to metaphor and paradox. Bolton (2005) suggests that within reflective practice "the narratives and metaphors by which we structure our lives, the taken-for-granteds, are questioned and challenged: making the familiar strange, and the strange familiar" (p. 109). Reflective practitioners are also encouraged to note paradoxes such as how our individual stories are tied to universal ones. Brookfield (1995) suggests that reflective practice helps us to realize that "what we thought were idiosyncratic features of our own critically reflective efforts are paralleled in the experiences of many of our colleagues" (p. 219). Most important, another purpose of reflective practice is to focus on, prioritize, and legitimize the importance of one's inner journey and to understand the need for connection and authenticity between what is happening in one's inner and outer life.

Although critically reflective practice literature is now emanating from most of the serving professions, teacher education has been the major locus of this literature. Increasingly, professions such as nursing and medicine are also embracing this genre of PD and scholarship. It is apparent that reflective practice has much to offer all the serving professions. For example, there is ample evidence of high attrition and burnout rates in the teaching profession (Darling-Hammond, 2003; Intrator and Kunzman, 2006). The possibilities that reflective practice offer for renewal and for potentially arresting attrition rates are significant. It is also widely known that workplaces such as schools can be very lonely places for adults to work, as they frequently do not allow for regular professional dialogue that goes much beyond anecdotal exchange and the trading of techniques (Cole, 1997). Yet despite gathering evidence about the benefits of reflective practice-based professional development, many employers still remain wary of it, often favoring more technical, skills-based, transmission and didactic types of professional development because they are shorter, cheaper, more exact, more easily accommodated with limited time and resources for PD, and more obviously linked to outcomes, and they are seen as "safer" because they do not risk crossing the personal–professional divide.

Reflective Practice and Professional Standards

Many professions have developed professional standards to explicitly state what qualified people in certain professions should be able to do, know, and practice. Apart from articulating specific skills and knowledge related to particular professions, most standards now also actively encourage reflective practice and self-knowledge, positioning them as legitimate and desirable components of professional practice. For example, in the landmark document *What Teachers Should Know and Be Able to Do*, the National Board for Professional Teaching Standards (NBPTS; 1989) listed Five Core Propositions, with one of them being that "teachers think systematically about their practice and learn from experience," and "critically examine their practice on a regular basis." These Five Core Propositions still form the cornerstone of NBPTS policy, and teachers continue to be encouraged and supported in being self-reflective.

A second example can be found in the Principals Australia propositions for educational leaders. Principals Australia (2005) has developed five propositions, known as The L5 Frame. The first proposition within this framework is that "Leadership starts from within" and that leaders need to be professionally self-reflective and to know themselves well. It suggests that leaders demonstrate this type of leadership by committing to the following:

- I take time to critically reflect on myself and my work.
- As a result of this reflection, I take action to look after myself.
- I articulate my beliefs and values and how they underpin my work.
- What people bring with them is valued as crucial to what and how they learn.

The Accreditation Council for Graduate Medical Education (ACGME) provides a third example. In 2007, the ACGME launched a book titled *Journey to Authenticity*, featuring stories of chief residents reflecting on their journeys as interns. The stories in this book exemplify a critically reflective approach to medical practice, in the ways the residents talk about why they became doctors, what they have learned about themselves and their profession, and how they have changed and grown along the way. In the preface, David Leach, 2007 Executive Director of ACGME, named the journey from intern to chief resident as a "journey to authenticity," which "actually proceeds from the inside out." He suggests that "paying attention to patients' stories enable residents to discover their own stories" and that "competence is the demonstrated habit of reflective practice" (ACGME, 2007).

Results from the Evaluation

The evaluation consisted of two components: an on-line questionnaire and interviews with participants and personnel involved in the development, and delivery of the Circle of Trust retreats. All of the forty-three people who had participated in at least two retreats were invited to complete the on-line questionnaire, and seven of the questionnaire respondents were also interviewed. In addition, five interviews were conducted with a selection of COT facilitators and CCR staff. The evaluation had an extremely high participant response rate, which seemed to reflect both the gratitude of respondents for their very positive retreat experience and their desire to give back to and remain connected with the Circle of Trust community. A total of 93 percent of those who were invited to participate in the evaluation responded, with 91 percent completing the on-line questionnaire. An unexpected but welcome outcome from this evaluation was the generative and positive outcomes experienced by participants as a result of participating in the evaluation. Respondents commented in both the questionnaire and interviews that the evaluation had provided a helpful catalyst for them to review, reflect on, and continue their Circle of Trust learning.

Overall, this evaluation was extremely positive, and respondents highly commended everyone involved in the development and delivery of the retreat program. It was evident that Circle of Trust retreats were highly

New Directions for Teaching and Learning • DOI: 10.1002/tl

successful, not only profoundly meeting participants' needs but exceeding their expectations. All participants were overwhelmingly positive about their Circle of Trust experiences and have widely and creatively applied their learning in both their personal and professional lives.

The Questionnaire. After examining the large quantity of data that respondents submitted in the questionnaire, it was clear that respondents were overwhelmingly positive about their retreat experiences, and they cited a large number of personal and professional applications from their Circle of Trust learning. Respondents were overwhelmingly positive about their Circle of Trust retreat experience. The vast majority (77 percent) reported that retreats were *exceeding* their expectations:

> I benefited far beyond any of my original reasons for attending. What I thought I needed was accurate but my expectations were exceeded as I also hoped for spiritual development and that was the greatest gift.

> It's the most powerful professional development I've ever experienced.

> It was what Parker described in *A Hidden Wholeness*, which was refreshing in a world which doesn't deliver what is promised.

Although each participant had experienced a different combination of Circle of Trust and CCR retreats, they nevertheless recognized, appreciated, articulated, and celebrated what they saw as the distinctive, common core of circles of trust. They described them as safe and trustworthy spaces where people can be alone within a community to experience silence, reflection, listening to their inner teacher, speaking into the circle, and clearness committees.

> The most distinctive part is the intentionality of the space—there are so few spaces in our lives that are held with intention. The safety and integrity that the Circle of Trust principles and practices are held with is remarkable and yet so simple.

Each participant expressed profound gratitude for his or her Circle of Trust retreat experience:

> I am grateful beyond words for what you have created that I have found.

> The Circle of Trust is a life-changing opportunity to reflect and revive the spirit. Thank you!

> Very powerful and important work is occurring through the retreats. Thanks for the opportunity to express the profound impact the work is having on my life. Keep them coming and let us expand the network of who can experience

the work as we listen for those hungry for this feast. Thanks for this—it is the most important work in the world and you are doing it

Circle of Trust was like water to a dying person. I was given life.

I think this is some of the most important work happening in education right now—it is essential work.

The quality of my work and life has advanced significantly each time I complete a retreat. It is as if I identify a key piece of who I am.

Respondents cited many personal and professional applications from their Circle of Trust learning. Regardless of their profession, respondents cited extensive examples of the ways in which they have applied their Circle of Trust learning in both their personal and professional lives. Although there was quite a deal of overlap between their personal and professional learning, there were also some different applications.

On a personal level, respondents cited their learning as including trusting their inner teacher, listening more fully, asking better questions, ensuring that groups are safe, rediscovering spirituality, inner healing, changing the metaphors that guide their lives, looking for paradoxes each day, and looking at themselves and others with "soft eyes."

I think my personal learnings are also my professional learnings.

I am now more focused, more intentional, more caring for co-workers, friends, family and others, more careful to take care of myself, physically, mentally, emotionally.

I have learned to listen better, to be more kind, to seek first inquiry, to listen to my heart.

I feel more at peace because I am more "me" than I have ever been in my life.

Coming back from the retreat, I noticed I was being even more careful with both framing and receiving questions.

I am experiencing a new world in which I am free to live congruently.

I believe through inner work learned at Circle of Trust Retreats I have become a better person for myself.

Best of all, I now have words and ways of "living divided no more."

On a professional level, respondents cited their learning as including engaging in deep listening, asking open and honest questions, having better understandings of group dynamics, holding safe spaces for people, practicing integrity, becoming a better teacher, not needing to fix workmates and clients, believing that people have the answers within, having more patience with big questions, using boundary markers, and using third things such as poetry in groups. Quite a few respondents reported that they are in the process of, or already have, set up a circle of trust in their own personal or professional communities.

I think I am now more comfortable and relaxed in my work.

The learnings have informed my leadership. I walk more lightly in the world.

My integrity will now guide my leadership rather than my leadership guiding my integrity.

I have returned to my community with a new approach to being in group meetings.

When working with people who come to me because of grief in their life, I am much more comfortable using the open questions and not feeling I have to fill up the times where no one says anything.

At the shelter, we are trying not to slip into fix-it mode when we are assisting our homeless guests. Instead of telling them what they need to do all the time (get a job, save your money, etc.) our staff now tries to ask our guests what they think they need and what they think would be helpful. This has really changed the entire atmosphere in the shelter and has really improved our guests' confidence and self-esteem.

I have learned how not to try and fix people all the time, to listen and ask clarifying questions.

I have been working intentionally with the Circle of Trust principles and practices in my consulting practice; trying to move beyond "fixing, saving, and setting straight" to a new kind of relationship with clients and colleagues, one that honors the identity and integrity of individuals, communities, and organizations.

My parishioners have told me that I seem more real, more at peace, and more personal. I feel that I have added skills for pastoral counseling through the knowledge of open and honest questions.

I just reread my journal, and can't begin to summarize all that I heard and felt and learned. Experiences from the retreats helped me to see what they have to do with courage and renewal. I have come to really believe in the process as an effective method of renewal.

Although the questionnaire revealed that respondents are overwhelmingly positive about their Circle of Trust experience, it is important to note that some also mentioned minor ways in which their experience could be improved (the most common suggestion was to make the retreats longer!). The majority of respondents, though, said that they could not think of anything that could be done to improve their Circle of Trust experience.

The Interviews

Semistructured phone interviews were conducted with seven respondents who volunteered to be interviewed in the questionnaire. The purpose of conducting follow-up interviews was to elicit more detail about specific areas of interest that emerged from the data received in the questionnaire. Notes were taken during the interviews, and the resultant data is presented according to two of the questions that interviewees were asked.

> Application of Learning. Can you please give me specific examples of how you have applied your Circle of Trust learning or experience to your personal or your professional life?

Interviewees indicated that they were already quite experienced in their own reflective practice, but deeply appreciated the opportunity to attend Circle of Trust retreats to extend and deepen this work. Each interviewee cited rich and varied personal and professional applications of Circle of Trust learning. The ways that interviewees are applying learning in their **personal** lives include:

- Placing an emphasis on invitation in their relationships.
- Asking open, honest questions. One interviewee commented that this was more easily done in professional life than in personal life, as personal relationships were more difficult to change due to ingrained habits and established ways of acting.
- Building in time during each day for intentional silence and reflection.
- Establishing circles of trust in their communities.
- Intentionally changing the metaphors that guide their life.
- Ensuring that the groups they are involved in are safe.
- Choosing to live life in a more humane way.

The ways that interviewees are applying Circle of Trust learning in their **professional** lives include:

- Establishing circles of trust in their workplaces.
- Setting up a reading group at work based on A Hidden Wholeness.
- Having a greater awareness of formation principles.
- Creating opportunities for an intentional dialogue process.
- Using third things such as poetry and art in their workplaces.

- Ensuring that the groups they are involved in within their professional life are safe.
- Changing the way they preach and what they preach about. For example, one clergy commented that he had recently preached a sermon titled "Life on the Mobius Strip."
- Becoming better teachers. For example, one interviewee commented that he connects more with his students on a personal level and that his students are noticing a difference.
- Changing both the practices and content of their teaching. For example, one interviewee described how she is using silence differently with her students.

Comparison to Other Professional Development. In your professional field, how do Circle of Trust retreats compare to other Professional Development that you have participated in?

All interviewees compared Circle of Trust retreats extremely favorably with all other forms of PD they had experienced. One interviewee said that the difference between Circle of Trust retreats and other PD was the "difference of night and day." Many people spoke about the ways in which Circle of Trust retreats enabled them to more fully integrate their personal and professional lives. Most interviewees felt that the major defining difference between Circle of Trust retreats and other forms of PD was found in Circle of Trust understandings about the soul, and the lifelong learning and applications that these understandings gave them. One interviewee commented that although "Parker Palmer didn't invent honesty or reflection, his understandings about the soul *are* new—such as the soul being a wild animal that is shy and not wanting to be fixed or saved." One interviewee commented that other PD and conferences she had attended were largely "didactic and deductive," with another saying that it was refreshing to not have "someone opening up the top of my head and filling it with knowledge."

Conclusion

This evaluation revealed that respondents were overwhelmingly positive about their Circle of Trust retreat experiences, with the vast majority reporting that these retreats were not only meeting, but *exceeding* their expectations. Most important, the evaluation revealed that regardless of profession, participants were able to extensively apply their learning from Circle of Trust retreats in diverse and myriad ways in both their personal and professional lives. Participants appreciated the way Circle of Trust retreats provide lifelong learning in reflectivity, presence, intentionality, self-awareness, listening, questioning, and group work skills. Participants also reported that they find Circle of Trust retreats highly distinctive and appreciate the ways that Circle of Trust retreats differ from, and more fully meet their needs than, any other professional development opportunities.

References

Accreditation Council for Graduate Medical Education (ACGME). *Journey to Authenticity*. Chicago: Accreditation Council for Graduate Medical Education, 2007.

Bolton, G. *Reflective Practice: Writing and Professional Development*. London: Sage Publications, 2005.

Brookfield, S. *Becoming a Critically Reflective Teacher*. San Francisco: Jossey-Bass, 1995.

Cole, A. "Impediments to Reflective Practice: Toward a new agenda for research on teaching." *Teachers and Teaching: Theory and Practice*, 1997, 3, 7–27.

Darling-Hammond, L. "Keeping Good Teachers: Why It Matters." *Educational Leadership*, 2003, 60(8), 6–13.

Day, C. "Professional Development and Reflective Practice: Purposes, Processes and Partnerships." *Pedagogy, Culture and Society*, 1999, 7(2), 221–233.

Intrator, S., and Kunzman, R. "The Person in the Profession: Renewing Teacher Vitality through Professional Development." *Educational Forum*, 2006, 71, 16–32.

Intrator, S., and Scribner, M. *A Longitudinal Program Evaluation of the Courage to Teach Program*. Bainbridge Island, Wash.: Center for Teacher Formation, 2002.

Knowles, M. *The Adult Learner: A Neglected Species*. Houston, Tex.: Gulf Publishing Company, 1990.

Loughran, J. "Effective Reflective Practice." *Journal of Teacher Education*, 2002, 53(1), 33–43.

National Board for Professional Teaching Standards (NBPTS). *What Teachers Should Know and Be Able to Do*. 1989. Retrieved July 1, 2011, http://www.nbpts.org/the _standards/the_five_core_propositio.

Palmer, P. *The Courage to Teach*. San Francisco: Jossey-Bass, 1998, 2007.

Palmer, P. J. *A Hidden Wholeness: The Journey Toward an Undivided Life*. San Francisco: Jossey-Bass, 2004.

Principals Australia. APAPDC L5 Frame: Building Leadership in Australian Schools. 2005. Retrieved July 1, 2011, http://www.principalsaustralia.edu.au/LLS_ FRAMEWORK.

JANET SMITH, Ph.D., is an educational consultant and associate professor at the University of Canberra, Australia.

NEW DIRECTIONS FOR TEACHING AND LEARNING • DOI: 10.1002/tl

INDEX

Academic Excellence Indicator System (State of Texas), 80
Accountability Ratings System (State of Texas), 80
Accreditation Council for Graduate Medical Education (ACGME), 104–105
ACGME. *See* Accreditation Council for Graduate Medical Education (ACGME)
Adams, F., 89
Allen, B., 1, 89, 93
American Academy of Poets web site, 41
American Red Cross, 95
Amini, F., 28–29
Amorok, T., 73
Arnett, J. J., 34
Aron, L., 28–29
Astin, A. W., 16
Astin, H. S., 16
Australia, 102

Balance, 58–59, 63
"Before" (found poem), 46–47
Berry, W., 7
Bess, J. M., 28, 29
Blomgren, R., 5
Bolton, G., 101, 103
Booher-Jennings, J., 81
"Both-and" thinking, *versus* "either-or" thinking, 7, 57, 61
Bounded space, 97
Bransford, J., 53
Brookfield, S., 101, 103–104
Brower, G., 1, 15, 16
Brown, B., 30
Bryk, A. S., 83, 85
Buechner. F., 64
Burd-Sharps, S., 93
Bussolari, C., 28
Butler, M., 28–29

California Marriage and Family Therapists, 28
Campbell, J., 71
Canada, 102
Cannon, M., 5–6
Catholic Educational Leadership (CEL) Program (University of San Francisco), 32

CCR. *See* Center for Courage & Renewal (CCR)
Center for Courage & Renewal (CCR), 1, 4, 14, 69, 89, 91–92, 102; formative values of, 97–98; and practices of Circle of Trust® approach, 12–13; and principles and practices of Circle of Trust® approach, 11; and principles of Circle of Trust® approach, 11–12
Center for Teacher Formation (CTF; now Center for Courage & Renewal), 69, 101
Chadsey, T., 1, 3
Chaos theory, 28
Chicago Annenberg Research Project, 83
Chickering, W., 16
Circle of Trust® approach, 1, 27, 95; in context of community recovery and democracy building, 91; for educators in changing times, 33–34; as informed by movement model of social change, 14; in Mississippi, 89; at Mississippi Gulf Coast Democracy School, 96; origins of principles and practices of, 5–6; practices of, 12–13; and practices that encourage shared exploration of self, other, and world, 8–9; principles and practices of, 3–9; principles and practices of, at work in world, 14; principles of, 11–12; principles of, at work in world of education, 9
Circle of Trust® approach, measuring impact of, 101–111; and history of Circle of Trust retreats, 101–103; interviews about, 109–110; questionnaire for, 106–109; and reflective practice and professional standards, 104–105; and reflective practice as form of professional development, 103–104; and results of evaluation, 104–109
Circles of Trust: creating, 37–39; cross-professional retreats, 102; dialing into, 37–51; programs, 78–79
Civil Rights movement, 92, 93
Clark, C. M., 54
Clearness Committee (Quakers), 6
Clinton, W. J., 94
Cole, A., 101, 104

Communal process, teaching and learning as, 3–5
Community, 97; inner work requiring solitude and, 11–12; lawyering, 95; principles for exploring inner lives in, 6–8; recovery field, 91
Community and Regional Resilience Institute, 91
Confidentiality, 30; honoring, 13
Conners, D. A., 1, 67, 74
Courage & Renewal Facilitator Preparation Program, 101–102
Courage & Renewal programs, 27
Courage to Lead® model, 69, 95, 102; and Courage to Lead® Montana, 39
Courage to Teach® (CTT) retreats, 38–39, 54, 69, 78–79, 101, 102
Courage to Teach: Exploring the Inner Landscape of a Teacher's Life (Palmer), 99, 101
CourageRenewal.org, 14
Cranton, P., 71, 77
CTT. See Courage to Teach® (CTT) retreats
Cycles, 12

Dalton, J., 16
Danielowicz, J., 53
Darling-Hammond, L., 53, 104
Day, C., 101, 103
Deep South, 93, 94
Diagnostic and Statistical Manual of Mental Disorders IV TR, 28
Dingfelder, S. F., 31
Dirkx, J., 71
Disciples of Christ, 39
Diversity, 97
Divided self, healing, 15–23; implications and considerations for, 22–23; participant experiences in, 18–22; soul-role dialogues in, 17–18; and vignette (five) of adjunct faculty, 21–22; and vignette (four) of tenured faculty, 20–21; and vignette (one) of university administrator, 18–22; and vignette (three) of pretenured faculty, 19–20; and vignette (two) of program staff, 19
"Downside" (found poem), 41

Edwards, J. K., 28, 29
"Either-or" thinking, 7, 57

Facebook, 33–34
"Failure of Logistics" (found poem), 43
Federal Emergency Management Agency (FEMA), 92
Fetzer Institute (Kalamazoo, Michigan), 39, 78, 85, 91–95, 101
Fink, D., 83, 85
Five Core Propositions (National Board for Professional Teaching Standards), 104
Floden, R., 54
Formation: as engagement with identity, 69; as engagement with integrity, 70; as retreat, 69; as seed of transformation, 70; and transformation, 69–70
Found poetry, 41–51; American Academy of Poets description of, 41
Foundation for the Mid South, 91–92; Resiliency Grants initiative, 95
Fox, J., 31
Freedom Schools, 92
Freitas, D., 22
Fuller, F. F., 53

Generosity of Spirit model, 95
Gladding, S., 31
Glasgow, A., 67
Gonzaga University, 1–2
Goodell, J. A., 1, 27, 28
Greenfield, S., 34
Greensboro College, 5
Group Therapy and Leadership class (University of San Francisco), 30
Guam, 32

Hansen, D. T., 53
Hare, S., 41
Hargreaves, A., 83, 85
Heart of Education: A Call for Renewal, The (Nepo), 4
Heifetz, R., 67
"Hidden wholeness," 12
Hidden Wholeness: The Journey toward an Undivided Life (Palmer), 11–14, 37, 40, 97, 102, 106, 109
Highlander Folk School (Tennessee), 90
Hill, T., 28–29
Hole, S., 58
Hope, 97
Horton, M., 90
Hospitable space, 97
Hoy, W., 85
Huebner, D., 53
Hurricane Katrina, 32, 89, 91–93, 95

Identity, 54, 55, 57; formation as engagement with, 69; role of, in transformational learning, teaching, and leading, 67–74

Identity, role of: and classroom simulation, 67–68; and difference between formation and transformation, 69–70; and simulation revisited, 69–70; in transformational learning, teaching, and leading, 67–74

Immigration and Naturalization Service, 68

"In Need of Needles" (found poem), 50

Individual and Family Development across the Lifespan class (University of San Francisco), 29–32

Inner teacher, 7, 11

Inner work, 11–12

Integrity, 7–8, 12, 54–57; formation as engagement with, 70

Intrator, S. M., 53, 69, 101, 104

"Irony" (found poem), 45

Jackson, M., 1, 3, 4, 78

Jackson, R., 78

Jacobs, D., 90, 92

Journey to Authenticity (Accreditation Council for Graduate Medical Education), 105

Journey toward an Undivided Life (introductory Circle of Trust retreat), 102

"Joy" (found poem), 47–48

Jurow, A. S., 78, 84

Kalamazoo, Michigan, 101

Katrina, Hurricane, 32, 89, 91–93, 95

Kegan, R., 72–74

Kitchenham, A., 77

Knowles, M., 101

Kohl, H., 54

Korthhagen, F.A.J., 53

Kunzman, R., 53, 69, 104

L5 Frame (Principals Australia), 104–105

Lahey, L. L., 41, 72, 74

"Lament" (found poem), 41

Lannon, R., 28–29

Lawrence, R. L., 40

Leach, D., 105

Learning, as communal process, 3–5

"Learning space" (Palmer), 97

Lesley University (Cambridge, Massachusetts), 41

Levitt, H., 28–29

Lewis, K., 93

Lewis, T., 28–29

Lindholm, J. A., 16

Linsky, M., 67

Living the Questions (intermediate Circle of Trust retreat), 102

Lopez, S. J., 28

Loughran, J., 101, 103

Love, 97

Love, C. T., 2, 37–39

"Loving the Question" (found poem), 46

Luskin, F., 28

Martins, E. B., 93

McDonald, J. P., 54

Meijer, P. C., 53

Mezirow, J., 71, 77–79

Michalec, P., 1, 4, 15, 16

Miranda, T. T., 1–2, 77

Mississippi, Circles of Learning in, 1; background to, 92–93; and collaborative approach to education-inside and outside academy, 94–96; and community recovery and rebuilding, 89–100; and community recovery frame, 91–92; creating conditions for democratic education in, 96–99; and what is being learned about transformation, 99–100

Mississippi Center for Justice, 91–93, 95, 96

Mississippi Gulf Coast, 92–95

Mississippi Gulf Coast Democracy School, 96

Mississippi Welcome Table Project, 94

Montana, state of, 39

Montana Courage to Lead®, 39, 51; and Courage to Lead for Clergy and Congregational Leaders pilot project, 39

Movement model of social change, 14

Muller, W., 56

National Board for Professional Teaching Standards, 104

NBPTS. *See* National Board for Professional Teaching Standards

Nepo, M., 4, 95

New Orleans, Mississippi, 92–93

Nieto, S., 54

Noordhoff, K., 1, 5, 53
Novice teachers, 57–59

"Occupational Transformation" (found poem), 48–49
"Old Maps" poem, 19
Oliver, Mary, 20, 21
One America Initiative on Race, 94
Open questions, 13
Open space, 8, 13
"Out of the Blizzard" (found poem), 44
"Over Many Miles That Separate" (found poem), 45

Palmer, P. J., 1, 3, 4, 6, 9, 11–14, 16, 17, 21, 29, 33, 37, 38, 40, 53–58, 62, 68, 69, 73, 74, 79, 89–91, 96, 97, 102, 106, 110
Paradox: appreciation of, 7, 12; and balance, 58; experiences during first year of teaching of, 61–62; experiences during program of, 60–61; meaning of, for novice teachers, 57–59; power of, in learning to teach, 53–64; power of, in teacher education, 63–64; and program context, 54–56; value of, to novice teachers, 58–59
"Parchment Boat, The" (Cannon), 5–6
"Paying Attention" (found poem), 49
Pendle Hill adult study center (Quakers), 6
Piercy, Marge, 21–22
Plodinec, M. J., r8
"Poetic inquiry," 41
Poetry, 21
Portland State University, 1, 5
Poutiatine, M. I., 1, 67, 69, 70, 74
Prendergast, M., 41
Principals Australia, 104
Professional Development course (Noordhoff), 54

Quakers (Society of Friends), 6

Reflection, multiple modes of, 13
Reflective practice: as form of professional development, 103–104; and professional standards, 104–105
Reflective Practitioner course (Noordhoff), 54
"Resource" (found poem), 51
Robinson, D. C., 27
Rothstein-Fisch, C., 85

Schlitz, M., 73
Schneider, B., 83, 85
School culture: educator questionnaire for, 87–88; positive, versus negative, 85
Scott, S. M., 77
Scribner, M., 101
Seasons Fund, 91–92, 95
"Self-role" paradox, 55, 56
Seligman, M., 28
"Seven of Pentacles" (Piercy), 19, 21–22
Sex and the Soul (Freitas), 22–23
Shirky, C., 34
Skype, 39
Smith, J., 2, 101
Smylie, M., 83
Snyder, C. R., 28
Solitude, 11–12
Soul-role dialogues, 16, 55; in higher education, 15–23
Stamm, L., 16
State of Texas Academic Excellence Indicator System, Comparison Group Data, and Multi-History for 2003–2009, 80
Steps Coalition, 91–92, 95, 96
"Struggle" (found poem), 48
SummerWest (University of San Francisco), 32, 33
"Sweet Darkness" (poem), 19

Tartar, J. C., 85
Taylor, E. W., 71
Teaching, as communal process, 3–5
Teleconference call, 41
Texas, state of, 1–2, 80
Texas Education Agency, 80
Texas Wesleyan University (Fort Worth, Texas), 78, 85
Time magazine, 33–34
"Time Together" (found poem), 42–43
To Know as We Are Known (Palmer), 90
"Tragic gap" (Palmer), 62, 68
Transformational learning: and nature of transformative process, _71–73; role of identity in, 67–74; structure for, 1–2; and teaching and leading for transformation, 73; and transformation as goal of education, 99–100; and transformative learning theory, 71–72
Transformative development, Robert Kegan and, 72–73
Transformative Professional Development retreats: learning about,

84–85; lessons learned from, 77–85; and overview of research results, 80–81; and overview of transformative professional development retreat space, 78–80; and significant results in positive school culture ratings, 81–83

Trumbull, E., 85, 93

Tucker, E., 1, 89, 93

United Church of Christ, 39

United Methodist Church, 39

Universal stories, exploring intersection of personal stories with, 13

University of Denver, 1, 4

University of Mississippi, 89, 94, 95

University of San Francisco (USF), 1; and Circle of Trust® approach and other on-campus activities, 32–33; Counseling Psychology MA program, marriage and family therapy emphasis (USF MFT program), 27; Department of Leadership Studies, 32; Dual Degree program for teachers, 33; Group Therapy and Leadership class, 30; Individual and Family Life Transitions Counseling, 31; infusion of Circle of Trust principles and practices into MFT program at, 29–32; Spirit of Educator class, 32; "Spirituality in the Workplace" group, 33; SummerWest, 32; Traineeship I and II classes, 31, 32

"Upside" (found poem), 44–45

USF MFT program. See University of San Francisco (USF) Counseling Psychology MA program, marriage and family therapy emphasis (USF MFT program)

Vanier, J., 56

Vasalos, A., 53

Videoconferencing, 39

Vieten, C., 73

W. K. Kellogg Foundation, 91–92

Wampold, B. E., 28–29

"Wednesday Morning" (found poem), 43–44

Welcoming the Soul and Weaving Community (advanced Circle of Trust retreat), 102

What Teachers Should Know and Be Able to Do (National Board for Professional Teaching Standards), 104

"Wild Geese" (Oliver), 20–21

Willett, C., 40

William Winter Institute for Racial Reconciliation, 91, 92, 94–96; core values and principles of, 96

Williams, T. T., 100

Winter, W., 94

Winter Institute. See William Winter Institute for Racial Reconciliation

"Woodcarver, The" (poem), 19

Zajonc, A., 16, 33

Zuckerberg, M., 33–34

OTHER TITLES AVAILABLE IN THE
NEW DIRECTIONS FOR TEACHING AND LEARNING SERIES
Catherine M. Wehlburg, Editor-in-Chief
R. *Eugene Rice*, Consulting Editor

For a complete list of back issues, please visit www.josseybass.com/go/ndtl

TL129   **Inquiry-Guided Learning**
Virginia S. Lee
Since the publication of the 1998 Boyer report, *Reinventing Undergraduate Education: A Blueprint for America's Research Universities*, inquiry-guided learning has been discussed widely in higher education circles. In fact, it is often summoned as a universal answer for various teaching and learning ills in higher education. However, many institutions adopt inquiry-guided learning even as they are struggling to understand what it really is. With eight institutional case studies drawn from colleges and universities in Canada, New Zealand, the United Kingdom, and the United States, this volume provides a clear description of inquiry-guided learning based on best practice. It also provides a window into the dynamics of undergraduate education reform using inquiry-guided learning, with a helpful final chapter that compares the eight institutions on key dimensions. It is a succinct and valuable resource for institutions attempting undergraduate reform through inquiry-guided learning, for practitioners and scholars of inquiry-guided learning, for instructors seeking good texts for courses on higher education administration, and for administrators seeking to understand and lead undergraduate education reform.
ISBN: 978-11182-99234

TL128   **Evidence-Based Teaching**
William Buskist, James E. Groccia
What could be more important to college and university faculty than teaching well? Indeed, the sheer output of empirical research on teaching and learning and the number of journals and professional conferences devoted to improving teaching reflects higher education's burgeoning emphasis on preparing its teachers to do their jobs more effectively. In the past several years researchers have not only investigated key variables influencing teaching and learning, they also have applied empirical findings to develop and refine new systems of teaching and learning—approaches that provide the infrastructure for the day-to-day organization and assessment of student learning over the course of an academic term. This volume of *New Directions for Teaching and Learning* provides an overview of these systems and offers an assessment of the effectiveness of each relative to both student learning and enjoyment of the learning process. The contributors are leading teaching scholars who have been responsible for much of the research, theory, and application of these systems to college and university teaching. These systems include the lecture, problem-based learning, case studies, team-based learning, interteaching, service-learning, just-in-time teaching, Web-based computer-aided personalized instruction, and online teaching. Each contributor outlines the basic principles of a system, describes how to implement the system, and reviews the empirical research literature with respect to the system's overall effectiveness in producing student learning and enhancing student enjoyment of the learning process.
ISBN: 978-11181-80686

TL127   Faculty and First-Generation College Students: Bridging the Classroom
         Gap Together
         Vickie L. Harvey, Teresa Heinz Housel
         The population of first-generation college students (FGS) is increasing in an
         ever-tightening economy, a time when employers demand a college degree
         even for an initial interview. According to a 2007 study by UCLA's Higher
         Education Research Institute, nearly one in six freshmen at American four-
         year institutions is first-generation. However, FGS often straddle different
         cultures between school and home, and many feel socially, ethnically,
         academically, and emotionally marginalized on campus. Because of these
         disparities, FGS frequently encounter barriers to academic success and
         require additional campus support resources. Some institutions offer
         increased financial aid and loan-free aid packages to FGS, but these
         remedies—although welcome—do not fully address the diverse and complex
         challenges that these students experience.
            Responding to these complexities, this volume's chapters extend previous
         research by examining the multiple transitions experienced by both
         undergraduate and graduate FGS. This volume's cutting-edge research will
         help college and university administrators, faculty, and staff work better with
         FGS through more effective pedagogy and institutional programs. Ultimately,
         this volume affirms how learning communities are strengthened when they
         include diverse student populations such as FGS and meet their particular
         emotional, academic, and financial needs.
         ISBN: 978-11181-42141

TL126   Self-Regulated Learning
         Héfer Bembenutty
         This volume reports new findings associating students' self-regulation
         of learning with their academic achievement, motivation for learning,
         and use of cognitive and learning strategies. Self-regulation of learning
         is a hallmark of students' ability to remain goal-oriented while pursuing
         academic-specific intentions in postsecondary education. Protecting such
         long-term and temporally distant goals requires that college and university
         students be proactive in directing their learning experiences, guide their own
         behavior, seek help from appropriate sources, sustain motivation, and delay
         gratification. The authors suggest how college students can control their
         cognition and behavior to attain academic goals, select appropriate learning
         strategies, and monitor and evaluate their academic progress.
            This volume calls the attention of students and educators to the vital
         role that self-regulation plays in every aspect of postsecondary education.
         The contributors provide compelling evidence supporting the notion that
         self-regulation is related to positive academic outcomes, such as delay of
         gratification, self-efficacy beliefs, and use of cognitive strategies, and that it is
         important for the training of teachers and school psychologists. The authors
         offer diverse vantage points from which students, teachers, administrators,
         and policy makers can orchestrate their efforts to empower students with
         self-regulatory learning strategies, appropriate motivational beliefs, and
         academic knowledge and skills.
         ISBN: 978-11180-91630

TL125 **An Integrative Analysis Approach to Diversity in the College Classroom**
Mathew L. Ouellett
College and university instructors continue to seek models that help
students to better understand today's complex social relationships. Feminist,
Queer, and Ethnic Studies scholars put forward compelling arguments for
more integrative understandings of race, class, gender, and sexuality and for
centering the experiences of women, people of color, and others traditionally
relegated to the margins. Intersectionality is one such approach.

In nine chapters, the contributors to this volume offer an overview of
key tenets of intersectionality and explore applications of this model in
faculty and instructional development in higher education. Gathered from
across the disciplines, they draw upon a range of approaches to social
identity formation, different theoretical models, and a complement of lived
experiences. When read together, these chapters offer a systemic approach to
change in higher education by addressing innovations at course, department,
and institutional levels.

Intersectionality does not advocate for a flattening of differences. Instead,
it argues for another layer of critical analyses that acknowledge the powerful
interplay of the many aspects of social identity to address the rapidly shifting
ways in which we talk about and describe identities in society and the
complexity of classroom dynamics in the academy today. By illuminating
the interconnected nature of systems of oppression, we shine a light on the
potential for disrupting the status quo and create stronger alliances for social
justice.
ISBN: 978-11180-27622

TL124 **Experiential Education: Making the Most of Learning Outside
the Classroom**
Donna M. Qualters
As the cost of education increases, endowments decline, and the job market
tightens, institutions of higher learning are faced with many challenges:
How do we remain relevant in a world where many still view us as the "ivory
tower"? If we bring in the outside world, how do we convince our own
faculty of its value in the classroom? How do we help students combine that
exposure with the deep reflection that will give them the knowledge and
skills necessary for their future?

Some of our most powerful learning experiences occur outside
the classroom. How should higher education institutions—and their
administrators, faculty, and staff—recognize, structure, encourage, and
supplement this direct engagement with productive work? This volume
addresses this question in the voices of veteran, passionate educators who
fervently believe in the value of learning from experience. Every day, each
of these authors incorporates extramural learning into their practice; in this
volume, they have contributed their insights into the forms of, issues within,
and operationalization of experiential education.

*Experiential Education: Making the Most of Learning Outside the
Classroom* is intended to aid administrators, faculty, and staff in the design,
construction, assessment, and funding of experiential education. From
descriptions of individual courses to the layout of entire programs, these
writers address the realities of experiential learning—the need to reflect
upon its lessons and engage colleagues in understanding its power.
ISBN: 978-04709-45056

NEW DIRECTIONS FOR TEACHING AND LEARNING
ORDER FORM SUBSCRIPTION AND SINGLE ISSUES

DISCOUNTED BACK ISSUES:

Use this form to receive 20% off all back issues of *New Directions for Teaching and Learning*.
All single issues priced at **$23.20** (normally $29.00)

TITLE	ISSUE NO.	ISBN

*Call 888-378-2537 or see mailing instructions below. When calling, mention the promotional code JBNND
to receive your discount. For a complete list of issues, please visit www.josseybass.com/go/ndtl*

SUBSCRIPTIONS: (1 YEAR, 4 ISSUES)

☐ New Order ☐ Renewal

U.S.	☐ Individual: $89	☐ Institutional: $275
CANADA/MEXICO	☐ Individual: $89	☐ Institutional: $315
ALL OTHERS	☐ Individual: $113	☐ Institutional: $349

*Call 888-378-2537 or see mailing and pricing instructions below.
Online subscriptions are available at www.onlinelibrary.wiley.com*

ORDER TOTALS:

Issue / Subscription Amount: $ _____

Shipping Amount: $ _____
(for single issues only – subscription prices include shipping)

Total Amount: $ _____

SHIPPING CHARGES:	
First Item	$6.00
Each Add'l Item	$2.00

*(No sales tax for U.S. subscriptions. Canadian residents, add GST for subscription orders. Individual rate subscriptions must
be paid by personal check or credit card. Individual rate subscriptions may not be resold as library copies.)*

BILLING & SHIPPING INFORMATION:

☐ **PAYMENT ENCLOSED:** *(U.S. check or money order only. All payments must be in U.S. dollars.)*

☐ **CREDIT CARD:** ☐ VISA ☐ MC ☐ AMEX

Card number _____ Exp. Date _____

Card Holder Name _____ Card Issue # _____

Signature _____ Day Phone _____

☐ **BILL ME:** *(U.S. institutional orders only. Purchase order required.)*

Purchase order # _____
Federal Tax ID 13559302 • GST 89102-8052

Name _____

Address _____

Phone _____ E-mail _____

Copy or detach page and send to: **John Wiley & Sons, One Montgomery Street, Suite 1200,
San Francisco, CA 94104-4594**

Order Form can also be faxed to: **888-481-2665**

PROMO JBNND